Translation and Nation

Negotiating "China" in the Translations
of Lin Shu, Yan Fu and Liang Qichao

Li Lu

Translation and Nation: Negotiating "China" in the
Translations of Lin Shu, Yan Fu and Liang Qichao
Authored by Li Lu

Canut International Publishers

Canut Intl. Turkey, Teraziler Cad. No.29. Sancaktepe, Istanbul, Turkey

Canut Intl. Germany, Heerstr. 266, D-47053, Duisburg,Germany

Canut Intl. United Kingdom, 12a Guernsay Road, London
E11 4BJ, England

Copyright © 2019, Canut International Publishers

ISBN: 978-605-7693-17-4 (Paperback)

About the Author

LU Li, PhD in comparative literature from the University of Massachusetts, Amherst, USA, Associate Professor at the School of Chinese Language and Literature, Beijing Normal University, and Research Associate at the Center for Literary Theory Studies, Ministry of Education of China. His research mainly focuses on translation studies, Marxist Aesthetics, and continental literary thought. His recent publications include: Literary Theory (by Paul H. Fry, Translation into Chinese) and several papers on major Chinese academic journals. He is currently working on a manuscript about the Non-representational turn in the humanities.

Address & E-mail: No. 19 Xinjiekou wai dajie, School of Chinese Language and Literature, Beijing Normal University, Beijing 100875, P. R. China; lli@bnu.edu.cn

Contents

Foreword by Briankle G. Chang

TRANSLATION... AD INFINITUM   *I*

INTRODUCTION   *1*
Identity Crisis and the Formation of Chineseness   *5*
Translation History of China   *13*
Translations of Lin, Yan, and Liang   *17*

1. CHINESE AS BLACK SLAVES:
LIN SHU'S TRANSLATION OF UNCLE TOM'S CABIN   *23*
Critical Reviews on Lin Shu's Translations   *23*
Translational Motives   *30*
Translational Methodology   *43*
Translational Techniques   *52*
Remarks   *58*

2. CHINA IN A NEW GEOPOLITICAL MAP:
YAN FU'S TRANSLATION OF EVOLUTION AND ETHICS   *61*
xin 信, *da* 达, *ya* 雅   *64*
Publishing Tian yan lun   *73*
Translation as rewriting   *88*

3. ALLEGORICAL NEW CHINA:
LIANG QICHAO'S THEORY OF
POLITICAL FICTION AND TRANSLATIONS   *103*
Xiao shuo, *Shōsetsu*, and Fiction   *104*
Translation and Political Fiction   *116*
Translating Newness in Science Fiction   *125*

4. CONCLUSION   *135*
Translation, Patronage, and Power   *137*
Translation, Mother Tongue, and Poetics   *143*

Bibliography

DEDICATION

To my wife Wang Li 王莉 and son Lu Anzhuo 吕安卓,
for their tolerance

To my father Lu Zhicheng 吕志诚 and my mother Wang
Zhiguang 王志光, for their love

Acknowledgements

TRANSLATION AND NATION: NEGOTIATING "CHINA" IN THE TRANSLATIONS OF LIN SHU, YAN FU, AND LIANG QICHAO

This book is aimed at examining each translation methods and strategies used by Lin Shu, Yan Fu, and Liang Qichao and, more importantly, exploring the contribution of their translations to the formation of a consciousness of Chineseness. I hope to show that rather than serving as a tool to literary history, translation during the late nineteenth and early twentieth century served as one of the most important tools for introducing new ideas and producing cultural changes. In chapter one, the author gives an historical account of the formation of Chineseness in the late Qing period and its current problematic status. Next, briefly introduces Chinese translation history, which still remains largely obscure to Western readers. Finally, the author provides readers with biographical information about the three Chinese translators and with a basic acquaintance of their translations. Chapter two starts with a review of the criticism of Lin Shu's translations. After a comparison of different translational motives behind Lin's first two translation projects, the author maps out a constellation of emotional, cultural, and commercial motives, suggesting that Lin Shu started his translation career in a turbulent era when new cultural paradigms and national consciousness were looming in the distance. Chapter three devotes many pages to Yan Fu's three translation criteria: xin 信 (accuracy), da 达 (intelligibility), and ya 雅 (elegance). The author argues that Yan Fu imbues these three ancient concepts with new meanings and tries to establish a new standard genre that is suitable to modern science. Though Yan Fu follows the original closer than does Lin Shu, he intervenes and manipulates the source text to the extent that his translation cannot be called literary translation. A study of Liang Qichao's theory of fiction constitutes the main part of chapter four. Liang Qichao promotes a completely politically charged literary genre to sharpen Chinese consciousness. The author also offers a comparison of traditional Chinese ideas of fiction and Liang's new fiction doctrine. Finally, the book examines Japanese influence on Liang's literary and political ideas. In the conclusion chapter, the author suggests that the three Chinese translators not only tested the plasticity of the Chinese language in accommodating foreign languages, but also destabilized the boundary within the Chinese language. By using an unfamiliar language to translate an unknown language, the three Chinese translators longed for a new Chinese language that would become the mother tongue of the Chinese people as opposed to other races and ethnicities.

Dennis Simon

October 2019, Berlin

Foreword by Briankle G. Chang

TRANSLATION... AD INFINITUM

Translation is fundamentally a matter of responsibility. Aside from the technical challenges such as word choice, syntactic renderings, style and like, that anyone working between languages inevitably faces, translation, understood simply as the movement of a text from its original home to a new context, is premised on the ability to respond to the call of languages in their dissemination and multiplicity. At the same time, inasmuch as translation is a question of responsibility, of the imperative to attend to the demand of a text's meaning as it travels across linguistic environments, it also brings to bear upon itself the question of inheritance. Since language—the *mater*, the matter, of our (mother) tongue—is given to us and, like a gift or love, is given for free and taken freely, we, as loving and speaking beings, cannot help giving our very being-in-language back to it, doing so, unawares perhaps, as to be the language's very own inheritor. "We inherit language," as Jacques Derrida says, "in order to be able to bear witness to the fact that we are inheritors," which is to say, "we inherit the possibility of inheriting," receiving, willingly or not, "as our share the possibility of sharing, and this is none other than the possibility of inheriting."* Language speaks to us first, and through its speaking, we speak back to it, to its sending that makes us who and what we are. In this sending and receiving, in this mutual address whereby the sender and receiver communicate their shared messages, language lives on, growing and continuing to grow against possible decay or uncertain death, that is, perpetually coming "into being as immediate sur-vival—and as "televised."** It is in this *communication*, in this coming together without there being anything in common for sure, translation—and with it the perils, the experiences (*ex-periri*), of speaking and writing—is born. Translation is born of language, and vice versa. There—somewhere unknown and before we are born—takes place a birth from and into which we are born, a birth televised from one speaker to another, from one text to the next, from one language to another, and back.

Since translation implies the multiplicity of language, by virtue of which one text can be considered original and the translation derivative or secondary, the difference between the two languages in question should be considered as the proper provenance, the virtual origin, the imminent medium, of inter-linguistic work. This difference constitutes the condition of possibility of translation, a condition that also makes translation impossible—not in the sense that translation fails to take place but because the difference that makes it possible remains irreducible. Thanks to this difference, translation is possible and impossible at once, for it falls short of being meaning-*full* to the target text and hence can only succeed, or give in to, itself by taking place again and again. Translation succeeds by failing and it fails so that it lives on.

---

* Jacques and Bernard Stiegler, *Ecographies of Television*, Cambridge, UK: Polity Press, 2002, p. 132.
** Ibid.

Translation is necessarily disappointing. Yet by failing to meet its appointment, that is, by falling short of being fully meaningful to the original, translation transforms the translator as much as the text being translated. Like the printing press or any translation software, translation brings two languages into a third text, thus teaching us how to (re-)read the given two, doing so "not by dissolving the authority of *one* language and substituting another one instead, but by demonstrating the principle of substitutability and repeatability. Translation brings about the dissolution of the fetish of originality," as Hamacher states.[*] Seen in this light, the oft-invoked remarks, "to translate is to betray (traduttore, traditore)," describes but the most common and basic of all inter-lingual affairs, suggestive at best of translators' noble and often painful struggle for fidelity to the original without offering any true hermeneutical insight. After all, no one sufficiently attentive to language and its varying and various possibilities would fail to recognize that betrayal is the singular gesture of faithfulness in the dimension of sense and sense-making, whose dignity can be compromised only if translation stoops to the technical triviality of finding equivalence between words and sentences.[**] Put simply, to translate is not simply to ferry the text-cargo to the other bank; it is to flow with and in the river (*riviere*) of language for the arrival (*ariver*) of its meaning that is to come (*a-venir*) and comes, when it does, only as passing ripples or vanishing traces. In translation there is little to lose and much to gain, not the least

---

[*]   Werner Hamacher, *Pleroma—Reading in Hegel*, Stanford, CA: Stanford University Press, 1998, p. 195.
[**]   We could mention here the remarks of Wittgenstein in *Philosophical Investigations* (London, Macmilan, 1968, 531): "we speak of understanding a sentence in the sense in which it can be replaced by another which says the same; but also in the sense in which it cannot be replaced by any other... In the one case the thought in the sentence is something common to different sentences; in the other, something that is expressed only by these words in these position.

that, as Walter Benjamin famously reminds us, we discover the possibilities of our own language as it travels.

Translation is in want of translation. However one reads this statement—as a declaration or report, as a demand or disagreement, as a principle or reproach—it suggests that translation is always *after* itself. Indeed, not only is translation in need of translation, it also exists only in translation, as traces and into the future. In translation, something new and foreign is undoubtedly made assessible, but this accessibility becomes assessible only under translation's conditions or presuppositions. Put differently, since every target text must have been translated in some way before it can become something translatable, since translation, as indicated earlier, dissolves the authority of the original and attests to the principle of substitutability and repeatability, every text translates all others, each being the beginning of an act that ends only to begin again. We may call this, recalling the title of Derrida's book on archive and Freud, *mal de traduction.** *Translate !* This is the imperative of language. And it is also the law of translation, provided that one recognizes that this law of translation is law only as another translation.***

In this book, aptly titled *Nation and Translation*, Lu Li responds critically to the demand of translation as it takes place between Chinese and major languages of European origin at the close of the seventeenth century when China began to "modernize" itself as a result of her encounter with the West. Rather than participating in the quasi-philological trifle over the adequacy of Chinese translations of foreign texts, Lu relates the practice of translation to the broad project of nation (re-)building that China found itself forced to engage in, when the force of Anglo-European

---

* Jacques Derrida, *Mal d'Archive: une impression freudienne*, Paris, Éditions Galilée, 1995.
** See, Hamacher, *Pleroma*, p. 204.

iv

expansionism began to weigh unbearably upon it. If nation, as is now widely recognized, is an "imagined community," if it exists from start to finish in the imagination of those who are gathered by its calling, then the image that calls and gathers must be first constructed and kept forceful discursively, namely, by a story-telling in and only in which nationhood stands as an attractive imaginary.*Central to his project—and this where the book's contributions lie—is Lu's effort and capacities to move beyond the horizon of narrative genealogies around nationhood to focus on the urgent and emergent practices of translation of Western classics by Chinese scholars facing the so-called " 西潮 (Waves from the West)." Through careful archival research and sensitive literary analytic procedures, Lu proves himself to be a true inheritor of Chinese letters: not only does this text charts an underexplored line of reflection underlying Chinese cultural modernity, but it also opens a critical perspective for understanding the relation between nation and narration, and by natural extension, the clash between civilizations characteristic of our world today. True to the meaning of the word "and" in its title, *Nation and Translation*, this book demonstrates forcefully the fact that inasmuch as nation must be translated without end, translation recalls inevitably the need for identity of every culture, every society, and indeed, every text, including this book itself and, perhaps, like others it promises to inspire readers to write. Translation is one of the responsibilities of (becoming) a nation and nation inherits the translations it performs on end. This book shows us that.

Briankle G. Chang

Professor of Communication, University of Massachusetts, Amherst, MA

---

* Benedict Anderson, *Imagined Community*, New York, Verso, 2016.

Introduction

In a controversial paper "Third-world Literature in the Era of Multinational Capitalism," American Marxist literary critic Fredric Jameson offers Lu Xun, the great modern Chinese writer, as an example to demonstrate his belief that "[in] the third-world situation the intellectual is always in one way or another a political intellectual" (2000:320). Based on the "three worlds" theory proposed by Frantz Fanon, Jameson makes an aesthetic distinction between first-world and third-world literatures and argues that "third-world texts, even those which are seemingly private and invested with a properly libidinal dynamic – necessarily project a political dimension in the form of national allegory: the story of the private individual destiny is always an allegory of the public third-world culture and society." (320; emphasis in original) Even though Jameson's proposition is not innocent of racism and imperialism, as Aijaz Ahmad forcefully and convincingly argues (Ahmad, 1987), there is some truth in his position. Studies show that modern Chinese literary history goes hand in hand with the formation of the modern China state and Chinese people (See *Hsia*, 1961; *Wang*, 1997; *Hanan*, 2004). During the process, every individual creative voice is politically charged and finally woven into a grand national narrative.

Compared with the extensive research on works created by modern Chinese writers, translated literature produced in China from the late nineteenth and early twentieth century has received little scholarly attention. The main reason for this situation has something to do with the conception of "translation" among most Chinese scholars. In the late Qing dynasty, translation was so loosely defined that it included paraphrasing, rewriting and adaptation. For various reasons, a majority of late Qing translators favored the free translation method and took liberty with the originals (See *A Ying*, 1955; *Guo*, 1998). If Lun Xun's idea of faithful translation was at odds with the fashion in the very beginning of the twentieth century, whether or not to be faithful to the original semantically and stylistically has become the focus when discussing a translations performed in the 1920s. Late Qing free translations were regarded as low quality translations and deserved little attention. The conception of translation as "faithful" copy of the original has dominated Chinese scholarship and prevented the study of the political, social, and cultural significance of Late Qing translations. This neglect is unwarranted; what makes a translation successful can be understood in several different ways. Since the 1980s, scholars such as Itamar Even-Zohar, Andre Lefevere, and Gayatri Chakravorty Spivak, have reviewed translation from different perspectives and brought us a variety of interesting findings. Regarding translation as a site of negotiation and struggle for national identity, postcolonial translation scholars have established a link between the rise of nationalism and the introduction of translated Western texts (See *Bhabha*, 1990; Niranjana, 1992). Polysystem theorists treat translated literature as a subsystem connected to other subsystems, among which exist dynamic relations. The new developments in translation studies provide new methods for studying translations of Lin Shu, Yan Fu, and Liang Qichao, the three prominent Chinese translators whose works prepared new genres, narrative paradigms, ideas, and subject matters for modern Chinese literature. My dissertation is aimed at examining each translator's translation methods and strategies and, more importantly, exploring the contribution of their translations to the formation of a consciousness of Chineseness. I hope to show that rather than serving as a tool to literary history, translation during the late nineteenth and early twentieth century served as one of the most important tools for introducing new ideas and producing cultural changes. In this chapter, I first give an historical account of the formation of Chineseness in the late Qing period and its current problematic status. Then I introduce briefly Chinese translation history, which still remains largely obscure to Western readers. Finally, I provide readers with biographical information about the three Chinese translators and with a basic acquaintance of their translations.

The three translators will be dealt with respectively in the following three chapters. Chapter two starts with a review of the criticism of Lin Shu's translations. Target-oriented criticism allows us to consider the cultural and political implications of Lin Shu's team translation method. After a comparison of different translational motives behind Lin's first two translation projects, I map out a constellation of emotional, cultural, and commercial motives, suggesting that Lin Shu started his translation career in a turbulent era when new cultural paradigms and national consciousness were looming in the distance. Finally, I examine closely the first part of chapter XIIIV of Harriet Beecher Stowe's *Uncle Tom's Cabin* and explore the translation methods used by Lin Shu. The conclusion I reach is that Lin Shu's translation of *Uncle Tom's Cabin* is politically driven, with additional considerations of marketability and literary fame.

Chapter three devotes many pages to Yan Fu's three translation criteria: *xin* 信 (accuracy), *da* 达 (intelligibility), and *ya* 雅 (elegance). Many critics take Yan Fu's criteria as the highest stage of a translation, but there remain huge differences among interpretations of each criterion and of the relationships among the three criteria. I argue that Yan Fu imbues these three ancient concepts with new meanings and tries to establish a new standard genre that is suitable to modern science. The first chapter of Thomas Henry Huxley's *Evolution and Ethics* is studied in order to explore Yan Fu's translation methods. Though Yan Fu follows the original closer than does Lin Shu, he intervenes and manipulates the source text to the extent that his translation cannot be called literary translation.

A study of Liang Qichao's theory of fiction constitutes the main part of chapter four. The chapter begins with Liang's advocacy of the political novel as a tool to illuminate Chinese people. Liang Qichao promotes a completely politically charged literary genre to sharpen Chinese consciousness. I then offer a comparison of traditional Chinese ideas of fiction and Liang's new fiction doctrine. Finally I examine Japanese influence on Liang's literary and political ideas.

In the Conclusion, some common translation methods used by the three translators are summarized. In addition, I offer my considerations on the cultural and political implications of late Qing dynasty translations. I argue that translated literature introduced to China not only new ideas and subject matters, but also new thinking paradigms that made imagining a Chinese nation in a global world possible.

Identity Crisis and the Formation of Chineseness

Chinese nationalism has become a hot topic both in China and in the West in the end of twentieth century. Western scholars and media have generally stressed the danger of Chinese nationalism as the manipulation of public opinions by the communist government. They have voiced their deepest concern about the high nationalistic sentiment in an authoritarian China and have worried that the phantom of xenophobia was returning from the boxers (see *Wei and Liu*, 2001; *Gries*, 2004). As a response, some Chinese scholars have made an apology for Chinese nationalism by critiquing Westerners' imperialistic prejudices. It is generally held that Chinese nationalism could accommodate values of freedom, democracy, and equality. Despite their different positions, both sides have tended to politicize the discussion of Chinese nationalism. I argue that Chinese nationalism is an un-finished identity formation project that started from the late Qing dynasty. Late Qing translations can be viewed as the aesthetic response to a Chinese identity crisis and an attempt to shape Chinese nationalism. To better understand late Qing translations, it is helpful to understand the identity crisis in late Qing period.

After the second Opium War (1856-1860) the great majority of literati-officials in late Qing dynasty became aware that the Chinese culture of thousands of years was undergoing an unprecedented change. As illustrated in a popular propaganda slogan "Get rid of the Manchurian barbarians, and restore the Chinese kingdom," the advocates of ethnic nationalism challenged the legitimacy of the minority Manchurian regime within the traditional demarcation between the majority Han Chinese and the non-Han minorities. As the second ethnic minority to dominate China and the Han people, the Manchurian Qing wisely claimed that Manchurians were the barbarian descendants of Han

Chinese. This strategy proved to be a success; Han intellectuals recognized the authority of the Qing as the successor of Chinese culture and regime. The situation changed when Chinese intellectuals attributed the failure of China in wars with Western nations to the fact that Manchurians were not authentic Chinese. Zhang Taiyan, the most important theorist of ethnic nationalism, contended, "If Manchus weren't wiped out, the patriotism of literati and countrymen wouldn't be cultivated. As a result, China would be exploited and encroached upon by European nations and America to a point that the Chinese people could be slaves of these countries" (*Zhang* 79). However, this appeal to a monoethnic Han China was doomed to fail in that the very concept "Chinese" traditionally was not so much an ethnic indication as a cultural designation. This culturalist perspective of Chinese nationalism finds a good demonstration in a debate about the status of Taiwanese literature the 1990s. In the debate, like late Qing translators, participants tried to locate or construct some sort of authentic cultural qualities in responding to identity crisis.

Since the rise of a worldwide anti-colonial movement in the 1940s and the acceptance of postcolonial studies in academia, it is not difficult to polarize the East and the West in order to empower and authorize indigenous voices. However, accessing the real voice of indigenous people becomes problematic because to appropriate ethnicity as the emblem of culture and identity has proven to be a dead end. The problem of "authenticity" thus came to cause much attention in cultural debates everywhere. In his study on modern Chinese literature, C.T. Hsia comes to the conclusion that modern Chinese writers, no matter within what genre they compose and what literary school they belong to, always expressed a kind of "obsession with Chineseness" in their work (*Hsia* 33).

The concept of authenticity suggests a strong sense of essentialism. In his seminal paper "The Work of Art in the Age of Mechanical Reproduction," Walter Benjamin stresses that the existence of an original essence is the prerequisite of authenticity (220). Orientalism, a typical essentialist epistemology in Western discourses, establishes the West's self-image of superior culture and the West's power over the East by authenticating the East as an unchanged and stable entity. As Partha Chatterjee shows in his book *Nationalist Thought and the Colonial World* (1986), many protagonists in anti-colonization share the same essentialist view of culture, nation, and race by retelling the same colonial experience through the perspective of the colonized. Theoretically, essentialism upholds the continuity and sovereignty of a tradition and culture, and insists on the homogeneity in that particular community. Essentialism has provoked many attacks since poststructuralism, postmodernism, and postcolonialism have reshaped Western academia. Anti-essentialism, associated with scholars such as Jacques Derrida, Michel Foucault, Jacques Lacan, and Edward Said, questions the ontological possibility of any categories of social existence. These anti-essentialist scholars, instead of searching for a static and fixed identity, which guarantees an authentic original of a culture, come to terms with a conception of a chaotic, multiple, and dynamic identity by contextualizing and historicizing identity. Not every scholar endorses fully the anti-essentialist critique. In his 2001 book *Becoming Japanese*, Leo Ching points out two problems with anti-essentialism. First, he argues that its view of essentialism as mere social and cultural constructions tends to dissolve all forms of essentialism. However, there exist in reality many specially essentialized forms of power and subjugation that to a large extent still regulate and delegate people's social activities. Second, anti-essentialism, according to Ching, fails to acknowledge the ideological connotation of essentialized categories (*Ching* 7-19).

The complicated nature of authenticity is revealed in the debate about the Taiwanese localization movement, first initiated by different understandings of Taiwanese literature. In her 1995 article "The Localization Movement in Taiwan," Chen Zhaoying divided Taiwanese literary history (since the occupation of Japan in 1895) into three periods of Anti-Japan (1895-1945), Anti-Westernization (1945-1983), and Anti-China (1983-) (*Chen* 67). Through this periodization, Chen Zhaoying was offering readers a historical account of the relationship between Taiwanese identity and Chinese identity. In the first period, Taiwanese, from the very beginning of the Japanese occupation of Taiwan, fought against the colonial policies of Japan by viewing themselves as an undividable part of mainland China, both culturally and politically. Even when most Taiwanese lost confidence in and felt angry at China's inability to reunite Taiwan, Taiwanese identity was not so much a sense of separation as a feeling of being part of the Chinese. This kind of overlap of Taiwanese identity and Chinese identity was the main topic of Taiwanese literature. In his famous novel, *The Orphan of Asia* (1946), Wu Zhuoliu, a representative of the first generation of Taiwanese writers, expressed "an instinctive feeling of belonging to China" (47). In the second period, the Kuomintang, or Nationalist, regime in Taiwan, depicted itself as the guardian of the traditional Chinese culture. Its aim was to transform traditional Chinese culture into local Taiwanese culture. Based on its efficient assimilation of the Taiwanese local residents to a broad concept of Chinese, Chen gives a positive evaluation of this task. While the Taiwanese local residents regard their culture as a different one, they also look at this different nature as a part of Chinese culture. This sense of responsibility for cultural guardianship reflected not only a conservative attitude toward the preservation of Chinese language, thought, and civilization, but also a resistance to Western thoughts, a decayed culture of industrialization and modernization. From the beginning of the eighties, an independent tendency was growing gradually, which finally led to the founding of the Democratic Progress Party in 1987, the first political organization in Taiwan claiming to build an independent Taiwanese country. Chen reads this independent identity as both a sign of ignorance of the history of Taiwan and a self-alienation of Taiwanese people.

Chen's survey of Taiwanese literary history draws strong criticism from the independent camp. Attacking Chen's essentialist method of identifying an absolute origin of Taiwan, in his refutation "The Tragic Mentality of the Chinese People," Liao Zhaoyang contends that the formation of Taiwanese identity was an ongoing process related to the pressure of mainland China. The long history of the Taiwanese obsession with Chineseness was not a history of identification, but a history of resistance by means of questioning and rejecting Chinese identity. He comes to the conclusion that "Taiwanese identity" is void. In "In search of Taiwanese Identity," Zhang Guoqing goes even further by foregrounding the voice of the indigenous minority peoples and asserting that only those aboriginal Taiwanese represent the real Taiwanese identity. After investigating the history of Taiwanese identity, he claims, "I am Taiwanese, not Chinese" (127).

Although Chen Zhaoying gives us a comprehensive and critical account of the development of Taiwanese identity, her attempt to pin down an authentic China causes her to overlook the importance of Taiwanese identity. Though she does not give us a definition of Chinese identity, her analysis suggests an unchanged Chinese essence with which the Taiwanese have identified. In this regard, identity is conceived as a pre-constituted entity in a chain of equivalence, existing in a cultural and historical vacuum. Taiwanese identity and Chinese identity are thus analyzed as distinct entities rather than as interconnected structures or systems in dynamic historical situations. Zhang Guoqing's view of the Taiwanese local residents as the authentic Taiwanese identity is trapped by the myth of authenticity. Instead of looking for authenticity in culture, Zhang hopes to discover some coherent selfhood in race and ethnicity. However, if this Taiwanese identity connotes a kind of singularity and exclusivity, then it is impossible to account for the diverse components of Taiwanese culture and ethnicity. I find Liao Zhaoyang's criticism of Chen's essentialism quite to the point. He notices that identity is a process of construction of selfhood through other's eyes, a process that is always mediated by the possession and dispossession of power. Through the powerful eyes of the mainland Chinese, Taiwanese identity constructs and defines an autonomy and self-determination for Taiwan. However, by emptying Taiwanese identity, Liao fails to acknowledge the ideological connotation of essentialized categories constructed on a more complex historical situation. The dynamic construction of identity does not necessarily mean that the identity is void of essence. Rather, it means some aspects of identity may shift with different others. Another problem with Liao's method is its sense of loss and solitude, a negative sense termed by Leo Ching as victimization. This victimhood, according to Ching, leads to a situation in which its political activity is locked in opposition to the hegemonic in a permanent bind (*Ching* 48). He also warns that the sense of being victimized can then easily convert to the kind of nativism that conveniently discards intermixtures, discontinuities, and fragmentation.

Ching provides us an alternative reading of authenticity by a close reading of Wu Zhuoliu's famous novel *The Orphan of Asia*. This story tells of a Taiwanese youth's search for homeland and Taiwanese identity. Situated in a historical and geographical triangle of China, Japan, and

Taiwan, Hu Taiming, the Taiwanese hero, tries to find a home for his spirit. On the one hand, though educated in Japanese language and culture, Hu never identifies himself with the Japanese and continuously fights against Japanese colonial power. On the other hand, Hu feels identified with Chinese culture and Chinese, dreaming of returning his spiritual home, China. However, when he goes to China to fight the Japanese, he is arrested on the charge of being a Japanese spy. At the end of the story, when he returns to Taiwan with the help of his Chinese students, Hu feels the Taiwanese are injured by nature. The notion of orphan, of being abandoned, of not belonging expressed in this novel has many different interpretations. For Chen Yingzhen, a famous Taiwanese writer who favors Chinese reunification of Taiwan, the orphan mentality is a channel through which a Taiwanese identity could be assimilated into a grander Chinese identity. On the contrary, for intellectuals favoring Taiwanese independence, the orphan signifies the very essence of Taiwanese identity, the sentiment of rejection and abandonment from both national (China) and colonial (Japan) representation. Unlike these two readings, Ching reads the orphan metaphor as a specific symptom of colonization expressed in the colonized's formation of consciousness, as an activity that attempts to account for the processes of cultural construction amid the colonial and national triangulation of Japan, China, and Taiwan. He concludes that consciousness is a function of knowing; identity is a static and determined existence. One of the ways to escape the determinism of identity struggles is to attend to the contingent processes of consciousness formation.

Actually, Ching's reading of the novel is a textual analysis of double-consciousness, a sense of always looking at one's self though the eyes of others. Taiwan has no static or fully constituted "identity." Rather, it must be understood in relation to the residual Chinese nationalism and the dominant Japanese colonialism. The state of being looked at is built into the way we look. On the one hand, the colonized culture constitutes its identity under the gaze of the dominant. On the other hand, the object status of the colonized culture becomes a predominant aspect of that culture's self-representation. However, the various perspectives about Taiwanese consciousness, completely conditioned by the political struggles in Taiwan, obviously lack the double-consciousness Ching provides us. Therefore, their discussions are pretty much limited to the categorical analysis, such as China/Taiwan, Chinese Han/ minority.

Postcolonial scholars, such as Edward Said, Gayatri Chakravorty Spivak, and Tejaswini Niranjana, observe that the rise of nationalism in nineteenth-century Europe owed a lot to Western translations of oriental texts. Fascinated by the complex relationship between translations of Western literatures and Chinese modernity, Der-wei Wang and Lydia Liu look at translation as a cultural transaction and attempt to uncover a "translated modernity" in modern Chinese literature. Translations of Lin Shu, Yan Fu, and Liang Qichao have attracted the attention of many scholars, but the relationship between their translations and Chinese nationalism has yet to be explored. The main reason for this is that translation is not regarded as a dynamic writing act conditioned by political, ideological, aesthetic, and literary considerations. Instead, translation is viewed only as a tool to fulfill a translator's political goal. While postcolonial translation studies encourages us to explore the impact of Chinese translations of Western text on the rise of Chinese nationalism, polysystem theory provides us with a functional analysis tool to expose the translation strategies used by different translators for different purposes.

Translation History of China

In order to show clearly the contribution of late Qing translators, in this section I offer a brief survey of translation history of China before I introduce translations of Lin Shu, Yan Fu, and Liang Qichao. Recorded translation activities in China date back to as early as Zhou dynasty (1122-221 BCE) when the Zhou kingdom was interacting with neighboring minority tribes. *Zhou li* (Rites of Zhou Dynasty) and *Li ji* (The Book of Rites), two of Confucian classics discussing rites, not only record official titles and positions for translators, but also explain the origin of translation:

> The people living in different regions of the country could not understand one another's languages. Their likes, needs and desires were all different. There were officers whose duties were to understand these people's minds and ideas, and communicate their likes and needs. These officers held the post of "ji" in the east, "xiang" in the south, "didi" in the west, and "yi" in the north.

> 五方之民，言語不通，嗜欲不同。達其志，通其欲：東方曰寄，南方曰象，西方曰狄鞮，北方曰譯。(*Ruan* 899)

> The duties of Xiang Xu were to receive the envoys from the tribes Man, Yi, Min, He, Rong, and Di, impart and explain to them the words of the king, so that a harmonious relation was maintained with these states. When the ambassadors or heads of these states came for an audience with the Emperor, Xiangxu would attend to diplomatic protocol and the use of diplomatic language, and would interpret for them.

> 象胥掌蠻、夷、閩、貉、戎、狄之國使，掌傳王之言而諭說焉，以和親之。若以時入賓，則協其禮，與其辭，言傳之。(*Ruan* 1338)

It is well accepted that there were three translation booms in the translation history of China before the May Fourth Movement in 1911. With the introduction of Buddhism into China in the first century, Buddhist ideas gradually gained acceptance among the Chinese. As a result, the first translation boom started in the Six Dynasties (222-589) when Buddhist monks set about translating massive classics of Buddhism into Chinese. Buddhist translation activities lasted into the Tang (618-907) and Song (960-1279) Dynasties. Since the translations were mainly on religious scriptures, rules and conventions were set for translators who should: "(1) be faithful to the Buddhist doctrine, (2) be ready to benefit the readers (Buddhist believers), (3) concentrate on the translation of the Buddhist doctrine rather than translating for fame" (Ma 45). The most notable monastic translators of this period included An Shigao 安世高 (active between 148-170), Dharmaraksa 竺法蘭 (232-309), Dao An 道安 (312 or 314-385), Kumarajiva 鳩摩羅什 (350-409), and Xuanzang 玄奘 (600-664). The translation of Buddhist works contributed to the spread of Buddhism, which would become one of China's major religions.

When the Jesuit missionaries approached China to spread Catholicism and teach science in the late sixteenth and seventeenth centuries, the second boom of translation began. This period lasted for a span of about 200 years. It was an age when science was gaining importance in the Western world. Trying to gain acceptance of the government and the Chinese people, Jesuit missionaries chose to introduce Western science by translation. Their translation of scientific works left its mark on the history of modern China. The most remarkable achievements during these two centuries were the introduction of such basic sciences as mathematics, geometry and astronomy (See *Xiong*, 1994).

At the turn of the twentieth century, in the late Qing dynasty, China witnessed the third peak of translating activity in its 3000 year long history, following the translations of Sanskrit scripts from the first century on and the massive translations of Western science and technology books initiated by Western missionaries from the sixteenth century on. Although these movements all exerted a huge impact on China by profoundly changing Chinese culture and mentality, the late Qing translation boom distinguished itself by several features. First of all, the amount of the translated books it produced, arguably, surpassed that of books written by the Chinese. According to an estimation made by A Ying, a well-known Chinese scholar specializing in traditional Chinese fiction, more than 600 titles of foreign fiction were translated and published between 1875 and 1911, and translations constituted almost two-thirds of the total, 618 out of 1170, ranging from political and educational novels to detective and sci-tech novels (1957:65).

Secondly, the translation activities were both government-sponsored and market-oriented. The failure of China in the second Opium War (1856-1860) marks the beginning of the Qing officials' reforms in education and political systems. Embarrassed by the lack of bilingual officials, the Qing central government established *tong wen guan* (Interpreters College), the first translator training school, at Beijing in 1862. To provide Qing officials with basic knowledge in dealing with foreign affairs, more than 200 titles were translated by teachers and students of this school, most of which were books of international laws and histories of Western countries. Some open-minded officials also established such language training schools at the local level. Influenced by an illusory recognition that Western countries only exceeded China in technology, translators focused their source texts on mathematics, chemistry, physics, astronomy, geology, agronomy, mineralogy, military technology, and manufacture. In addition to the government-sponsored translations, the thriving private publishing houses greatly facilitated development of translation of Western literature by financially supporting translators. With the rapid commercializing trend at port cities like Guangzhou and Shanghai, newspapers and magazines were issued in an accelerating pace to meet the reading needs of urban residents. According to A Ying, translations of Western literature literally appeared in every issue of literary magazines, and some of them published only translation works (1955:187). Due to the marketability of fiction, publishers hired and paid well translators to rewrite, paraphrase, and translate Western fiction.

Thirdly, the blossoming of the translation of Western literatures during the late Qing period was concomitant with the rise of Chinese nationalism. In contrast to the European nations on which Benedict Anderson bases his observations, China remained a unified kingdom with vast territory, various ethnicities, and long cultural history. According to the traditional Han Chinese view, *Zhongguo* (China), meaning the central kingdom, is the world's geographical and civilized center surrounded by different barbarians. The position of a barbarian people is judged by the extent to which they are assimilated to the Han Chinese culture.

This idea of Chinese-centrism had not faced any serious challenge until the dying Qing Empire confronted the European colonizers in the nineteenth century. The relationship between China and Western powers cannot be accommodated by the traditional binary of Chinese and barbarian. The crisis of Chinese identity forced many Chinese to find new sources of identification from an ethnic or cultural stance that accordingly formed different types of nationalism. Translation played a key role during this time of transition.

Translations of Lin, Yan, and Liang

In 1978, Even-Zohar first introduced the idea "polysystem" for the aggregate of literary systems. In "The Position of Translated Literature within the Literary Polysystem", Even-Zohar points out:

> Translated works do correlate in at least two ways: (a) in the way their source texts are selected by the target literature, the principles of selection never being uncorrellatable with the home co-system of the target literature (to put it in the most cautious way); and (b) in the way they adopt specific norms, behaviors, and policies – in short, in their use of the literature repertoire – which results from their relations with other home co-systems. There are not confined to the linguistic level only, but are manifest on any selection level as well. (45)

It is clear that he tries to treat translation as a complex and dynamic activity governed by systematic relations rather than by *a priori* fixed parameters of language capabilities.

Gideon Toury extended Even-Zohar's theory by a more detailed consideration of the role of "norms" in the translation process. He regards the main goal of translators as to achieve acceptable translations in the target culture. Translations for him are "facts of the culture which receive them. The concomitant assumption is that whatever their function and identity, they are constituted within the same culture and reflect its own constellation" (*Toury* 24). Since translators do not work in ideal and abstract situations, they manipulate the source text to inform as well as conform to existing cultural constraints.

One of the merits of Even-Zohar's polysystem theory is its macro-perspective on translation that makes it possible, and necessary, to bring in cultural, political, and economic factors to study translation. From the point of view of structuralism, Even-Zohar treats literature as a huge synchronic and diachronic system that contains numerous correlated small subsystems of which translated literature is a particular one. This hypothesis not only changes the prevailing concept of translated works as individual, closed texts, but leaves enough space for many significant but overlooked questions about translation strategies, norms, receptions, and functions.

But at the time he proposed his theory, translation studies was still under the influence of various scientific tendencies. He anticipated that "it is necessary to include translated literature in the polysystem. This is rarely done, but no observer of the history of any literature can avoid recognizing as an important fact the impact of translations and their role in the synchrony and diachrony of a certain literature" (*Even-Zohar* 15). My study examines translated literature in the Chinese context within the framework of Even-Zohar's theory. The importance of Yan Fu, Lin Shu, and Liang Qichao in modern Chinese literature and culture is well recognized. I discuss their translations in the following chapters.

Having studied naval science in England for four years, Yan Fu (1853-1921) not only acquired a good command of English, but also exposed himself to modern Western thought by extensively reading books of political science. In the wake of the humiliating defeat of the Qing in the Sino-Japanese War (1894), Yan Fu started his translation career in order to find China a road to wealth and power. He can be credited for having translated T. H. Huxley's *Evolution and Ethics* (1897), Adam Smith's *An Inquiry into the Nature and Causes of the Wealth of Nations* (1898-1900), Edward Jenks's *A History of Politics*, John Stuart Mill's *On Liberty* (1898-1900) and *System of Logic* (1905), Charles de Montesquieu's *De l'Esprit des Lois* (1904), and Herbert Spencer's *Study of Sociology* (1903).

Besides his painstaking translation work, Yan Fu also contributed to translation theory. In his 1897 translator's preface to *Evolution and Ethics*, Yan Fu proposed his influential criteria of good translation: *xin* (fidelity), *da* (comprehensibility), and *ya* (elegance) (*Yan* 1321). Despite different interpretations and controversies on the real meaning of each concept, this claim was so powerful that these three requirements functioned as the translational norms in China for years. However, Yan's norms of translation were less authoritative and dominant for his contemporaries than what scholars might think. Yan's contemporary Chinese translators developed, applied, and introduced many strategies in their translations, taking into consideration factors such as readership, fashions, and contingent needs.

If Yan Fu provoked the mind of the Chinese intellectuals, Lin Shu (1852-1924) touched their heart with his translations of Western novels. Between 1899 and 1924, Lin Shu translated into Chinese as many as 180 titles of English, French, Russian, American, and Spanish as well as other literatures. The works he translated included Cervantes' *Don Quixote* (1922), Daniel Defoe's *Robinson Crusoe* (1905), Jonathan Swift's *Gulliver's Travels* (1906), Sir Walter Scott's *Ivanhoe*, Stowe's *Uncle Tom's Cabin* (1901), Victor Hugo's *Quatre-vingttreize*, Alexandre Dumas' *La Dame aux caméllias* (1899), Leo Tolstoy's *Caucasian Prisoner* (1920), Henrik Ibsen's *Ghosts* (1921), Washington Irving's *Sketch Book* (1907), and a lot of the writings of Charles Dickens and Rider Haggard.

Lin Shu, however, knew no language other than Chinese. Working with his language proficient collaborators who paraphrased the source texts, Lin rewrote those oral renditions in his elegant classical Chinese. Because of the limits of team translation, Lin's translations were unavoidably free ones and a domesticating strategy was his primary choice.

Lawrence Venuti's observation is basically true when he claims that Lin Shu "chose foreign texts that could be easily Sinicized, assimilated to traditional Chinese values, notably the archaic literary language and family-centered Confucian ethics" (179). However, the complexity lies in the contradiction between Lin as a thinker, whose drive to translation was to educate Chinese people and reform the imperial country, and Lin as a popular translator, who had to cater to readership and consider marketability.

Liang Qichao (1873- 1929) was among the more open-minded Chinese intellectuals who were shocked by the defeat of China in the first Sino-Japanese War (1894-1895), and who immediately engaged in political actions to reform or revolt against the Qing kingdom. He actively participated in the Hundred-day Reform (1897), the goal of which was to modernize the political systems in China with the support of young Emperor Guangxu, and was exiled to Japan after the failure of the reform. Realizing the potential political and social impact of the newspaper, he founded *Shi Wu Bao* (Current Affairs) and *Xin Min Cong Bao* (New People) in Shanghai. He reserved space in them for translations and writings of fiction. The special status of Liang Qichao as both a patron and a translator allowed him to take a more radical and violent attitude towards readers. Since fiction was a tool to educate and enlighten, Liang assumed that the majority of its readership was il-literate, whom Liang usually called fools. In terms of this asymmetrical relationship, Liang introduced the political novel, a completely new literary form that might destroy Chinese readers' reading conventions, as the political novel did not account for its domesticating strategy regarding form and structure. In the preface to his 1902 political novel, *The Future of a New China*, he described its style as being "like a novel, but not really; it was like a history, but not really; it was like a criticism, but not really. I don't know what genre it is" (*Chen* 38). To achieve his political aim to educate people, Liang destabilized the traditional conventions of fiction and radicalized the subject and content.

In the following chapters, I examine each translator's special translation methods and strategies by closely reading their translation excerpts of considerable length, and point out how their translations contributed to the evolution of Chinese literature, which, in turn, led to a change in the conception of Chinese cultural identity.

Chapter One

CHINESE AS BLACK SLAVES: LIN SHU'S TRANSLATION OF **UNCLE TOM'S CABIN**

Critical Reviews on Lin Shu's Translations

Recent studies show that Lin Shu's translation legacy consists of more than 180 translations of literary works written by various western authors. Out of controversies over how to assess the huge bulk of works, both Chinese and foreign scholars unanimously agree upon one thing, namely, Lin's translations are free translations as opposed to literal translations. By free translations, scholars mean that Lin Shu "at will deletes and edits the source texts" (*Zheng* 1226). Most of the scholars who criticize Lin Shu hold to the belief that translations should be faithful to the original with as few lexical or syntactical deviations as possible. In his dissertation, Robert Compton goes so far to assert that: "In the strictest sense of the word, Lin Shu was not a translator at all" (132). Lin must have felt the great pressure from this criticism even in his lifetime. In 1908, he concluded an epilogue to a new translated novel with this disclaimer:

> Recently my close friends from within the seas wrote to me. In the letters they listed mistakes in my translations for my review. I really appreciate it! However, I don't know any western languages. What I did was just write down the oral renditions [made by my collaborators]. Even if there were mistakes, I didn't know.

> 近有海內知交投書，舉鄙人謬誤之處見箴，心甚感之。惟鄙人不審西文，但能筆述，即有訛錯，均出不知。 (*Xiliya jun zhu bie zhuan* 1)

Lin Shu suggested that his collaborators needed to take the blame for any mistreatments to the original. In a move apparently to appease the anger of his collaborators, Lin five years later conceded that: "As for the mistakes, they are due to my carelessness and absent-mindedness. This is all my fault and has nothing to do with my friends" (Ma 427).

Although aware of Lin's later explanation, most scholars still hold Lin's collaborators alone accountable for the shortcomings of Lin's translations. In his 1924 article "Lin Qinnan xian sheng" 林琴南先生 (Mr. Lin Shu), the first full-length article devoted to Lin Shu's contributions to translation and Chinese literature, Zheng Zhenduo (1898-1958), a leading literary critic at the time, surveyed all the translations he could collect. One of his important findings was that the texts of two thirds of Lin's translations were second- and third-class literary works, which contained so little literary value that Lin should not have translated them. He also noticed that Lin Shu deleted the source texts and added in the translation portions he made up. Interestingly, Zheng attributed these to the low literary taste and linguistic incompetence of Lin's collaborators. He claimed that "If he [Lin Shu] had had several good collaborators, his achievements in translation should have been made much better than this" (161). Paradoxically, Zheng categorized Lin Shu as a salient faithful translator in his time when free translation was popular, for Lin was good at replicating the original tone and was faithful to original titles and personal and geographic names. Collaborators' roles were not mentioned at all in this respect.

In 1935, Hanguang published *Lin Qinnan* 林琴南, the first monograph on Lin's life, political thought, literary creations, translations, and achievements in arts. Of the seventeen conclusions the author reached through his comprehensive study, all three negative remarks were related to his translations. On the one hand, Hanguang viewed Lin Shu's inability to read any foreign language as his weakest point; on the other, he asserted that collaborators alone should be responsible for the problems in Lin Shu's translations (86-7).

Until very recently, this kind of source-oriented perspective has dominated the way in which a translation is viewed and evaluated in general, and how Lin Shu is treated in particular. No matter how hard some translation critics have tried to neutralize the distinction between free translation and literal translation, the hierarchic tension intrinsic to any binary relationship always foiled their attempts to give a balanced picture of Lin Shu, the most prolific translator in China, who however did not know any foreign language. The solution to this interpretational predicament is to be found in the target- and culture-oriented trend that gradually gained momentum in the "manipulation school" and within polysystem theory in the past decades. Instead of scrutinizing translators' linguistic or philological competence and aiming to achieve a (dynamic) equivalent translation, critics influenced by this new trend are mainly concerned with the different strategies employed by translators in order to negotiate cultural differences between the source text and the target text. Andre Lefevere's idea of translation as a kind of rewriting is of particular importance to our re-evaluation of Lin Shu's translations. In his book *Translation, Rewriting and the Manipulation of Literary Fame* (1992), Lefevere argues that rewriting sets both ideological and poetological constraints for literature and plays a dominant role in the literary evolution. Among many forms of rewriting, such as translation, historiography, anthologization, criticism, editing, and adaptation, he believes that translation is the most "obviously recognizable" and "most influential" type of rewriting, since translation projects "the image of an author and/or a (series of) work(s) in another culture, lifting that author and/or those works beyond the boundaries of their culture of origin" (9). By locating a translation within the ideological milieu of its era, Lefevere intends to explain how the translation manipulates its original politically and poetically. In terms of political factors, he gives much attention to patronage, a power that operates outside the literary system but can "further or hinder the reading, writing, and rewriting of literature" (15). Patronage provides translators with political protection, financial support, and the reward of fame, while translators in return work within the ideological constraints set by their patrons. Thus, the dynamic relations between the translator and his patron are worth serious study. New questions therefore need to be raised regarding Lin Shu's translations: Who chooses the text to translate? What are the motives to translate? How exactly does a team translation proceed? Why did Lin Shu use classical Chinese in his translations? How did he and his collaborators resolve translation problems related to cultural factors? Besides linguistic incompetence, what accounted for Lin Shu's mistranslations, deletions, edition, and adaptations? Who were his target audience? Through what channel did he publish his translations? Did any individuals or any institutions sponsor Lin Shu's translations?

Some scholars have addressed those questions and reached many fascinating conclusions. Qian Zhongshu's "Lin Shu de fan yi" 林紓的翻譯 (Lin Shu's Translations, 1979) is the most influential essay that studies the characteristics of Lin Shu's translations from a dialectical perspective. Echoing to some extent the deconstructive approach to translation, Qian Zhongshu (1910-1999) started his analysis with a play on the word of *yi* (to translate). He pointed out that translation always functions at the same time as a seduction (to read the original), a matchmaker or medium, a misunderstanding, and a transformation. Based on his personal reading experiences of Lin's translated novels, Qian provides us with insightful remarks on the conflicting nature of Lin Shu as translator: his translations tend to erase as well as preserve themselves. Lin's translations opened up a literary world distinctively different from Chinese literature, which was very appealing to the Chinese readers who knew nothing about foreign languages and literatures. Compelled by either a desire to learn or a nationalistic urgency for survival, readers like Qian became enthusiastic to explore the knowledge of other cultures. Lin's notorious free style of translation therefore dissuaded those knowledgeable readers from reading his translations, and then his popularity came to an end. Qian concludes that both Lin Shu and his collaborators were responsible for mistranslations, but they made different kinds of mistakes. Qian made a distinction between missing errors and adding errors in Lin's translations. Through a close reading, he discovered that Lin's collaborators usually made errors such as missing passages and words, which led to inconsistency in the translation. Equipped with a sense of confidence in his literary abilities and a sense of superiority over the original authors, Lin Shu invariably added his own creations or rearranged the original. The reason behind it was his attempt to enhance the quality of the original. Using Lin Shu as an example, Qian Zhongshu's article gives an account of the historical situation when the domesticating strategy of translation was popular in the Chinese context. More importantly, his approach to translation studies embraces elements of both target-oriented and deconstructionist approaches to translation.

Though every western scholar who studies modern Chinese literature understands the importance of Lin Shu, there are few monographs in English on Lin Shu's translations. Arthur Waley, the famous translator of Chinese literature into English, may be the first western scholar to give Lin Shu's translations a serious review. Arthur Waley's translations of Chinese literature were often criticized by commentators as taking too much liberty with the original to order to meet his aesthetic tastes. He must have found in Lin Shu's translations his ideas on translation. He recognized Lin Shu as one of the greatest early nineteenth-century translators and viewed his translations as a means to re-revolutionize Chinese culture. In his "Notes on Translation," he gives a wonderful analysis of Lin Shu's use of classical Chinese in translating Dickens:

> To put Dickens into classical Chinese would on the face of it seem to be a grotesque undertaking. But the results are not all grotesque. Dickens, inevitably, becomes a rather different and to my mind a better writer. All the overelaboration, the overstatement and uncurbed garrulity disappear. The humor is there, but is transmuted by a precise, economical style; every point that Dickens spoils by uncontrolled exuberance, Lin Shu makes quietly and efficiently. (69)

His argument is not based on the categorical binary between literal translation and paraphrase. On the contrary, he regarded Lin Shu as a transmitter who introduced European fiction to China.

R. W. Comption, as mentioned before, wrote the first dissertation on Lin Shu in the West, but his basic evaluation of Lin Shu's translations was low and negative. Conceding that Lin Shu played a major role in the literary scene of modern China, Compton deems his contributions to be minor since his translations have ceased to circulate widely since his time. Influenced by mainstream Chinese scholars, Compton focused his attentions on Lin Shi's conservative and traditional thought and activities. He believed that Lin Shu's translations of Western literature should be seen as "an attempt to uncover sources of inspiration or new ideas which might be incorporated into the Chinese literary tradition" (99-100). His work has some merits. Compton gives us a biography of Lin Shu in English, which has helped western readers to learn more about Lin Shu's life. He also documented every one of Lin Shu's collaborators and listed all the titles they worked on with Lin.

Overseas Chinese scholars have made important contributions to Lin Shu scholarship and have deepened our understanding of Lin Shu's translation practices. As early as 1965, Leo Ou-fan Lee took Lin Shu's translation as the subject of a monographic study. After he examined Lin's translations through the subject matter of sentiment, ethics and adventure, Lee acclaimed Lin Shu as one who "stands out as a pioneering genius who for the first time introduced a considerable volume of western literature into China" (159). In Lee's view, Lin not only brought Chinese intellectuals to reconsider the importance of fiction as a genre, but also opened the eyes of his Chinese readers to see the real world. The influence of Lin's translations on the development of modern Chinese literature was documented and was given a high appraisal.

Translational Motives

China's humiliating defeat by Japan in 1895 was of great significance in modern Chinese history. The sense of humiliation gave rise to a sense of the Chineseness as a race and Chinese nationalism. The boom of the translation of Western social and political works and literatures was a concomitant phenomenon. It is well known that Lin Shu was very loyal to the Qing court, especially to Emperor Guangxu, and had a strong nationalistic sentimentality. Enough evidence has been offered to show that there existed a dynamic relationship linking the socio-political situation in China, Lin Shu's early translations, and the popular psyche of the Chinese people. Zhu Xizhou, one of Lin Shu's students and a painter, edited an anthology of Lin's works and wrote several articles describing Lin Shu's life. In his 1949 book *Chunjue zhai zhu shu ji* 春覺齋著述記 (Accounts of Works in the Studio of Awakening Spring), he made a comment about Lin:

> Master Lin is full of passions; his caring for and worrying about the common people, his loyalty to the court and his love for the country, are his natural feelings. Therefore, whatever stimulates his heart, he will express it with his brush. Among his works, the preface to *Ai guo er tong zi* (Two Children Who Love Their Country) is a piece of writing with blood and tears. His translations contain topics regarding loyalty and piety, politics, adventure, pleasure of love, and heroic deeds, detective story, and humor. The aims of every translation are to reform the society and the country and to encourage and exhort his fellowmen to improve. As for promoting Western literatures, it is only an auxiliary achievement.
>
> 先生生富熱情，憂閔忠愛，出自天性，故觸感輒發，其愛國二童子達旨之篇，尤為血淚

文章。其餘所譯孝義、政治、志怪、探險、以
及男女愛悅之情，傖荒俠烈之行，偵探滑稽之
事，且無一不寓革新國社，激勸世人之微意，
而表章西人文學，又其餘興也。 (*Zhu* v.2 3)

The logic of the dynamic relationship is evident in this passage: the social and political situation motivated Lin Shu to write and translate, through which he expressed his patriotic emotion. As a result of the popularity of his translations, Lin Shu influenced Chinese people with this nationalistic sentimentality.

From the point of view of translation, many questions still remain unanswered: Was the political agenda the only motive for Lin to translate? How did Lin find a source text suitable to this agenda? How did Lin work with his collaborators? Did Lin appropriate the source text to meet his political expectations? Did his collaborators influence his reading of the source text? Besides the obvious influence of his translations on readers, did the expectation of readers influence Lin's choice of source text and translation strategies? In the following sections, in order to give a more subtle account of the process and strategies of Lin's translations, I attempt to answer some of these questions by comparing Lin's different motives to translate and by comparing his stated translation ideas and his translation practice exemplified in translating *Uncle Tom's Cabin*.

In an oft-cited epilogue, Lin Shu made it very clear that "to cultivate patriotism and preserve the [Chinese] race" was the sole motive in translating *Uncle Tom's Cabin*, his second translation project. In a sense of urgency, he went on to describe the intention of this translation: "The reason that I and Mr. Wei [Yi] worked together to translate this book was not that we took the advantage to narrate a tragedy to win sympathetic tears from the readers, but that the danger of being enslaved is coming close to our

race. So we have to cry out to wake up our fellow people"
(104). More conspicuously, in the preface and epilogue, the
miserable conditions of Chinese laborers in America were
repeatedly compared with those of black slaves described
by Harriet Beecher Stowe. In the preface, he writes:

> The yellow race has been subject to worse treat-
> ment than even the black. ... I noted what the book
> relates about the Negroes and when I reflected that
> the yellow race too are facing subjugation, my indig-
> nation increased. ... Some Chinese think too well of
> the white race and, believing that Western powers
> treat their vassal states leniently, are actively campa-
> igning for affiliating with them. To such people, this
> book I have translated ought to serve as a necessary
> warning.

> 黃人受虐，或加甚於黑人... 觸黃種之將
> 亡，因而愈生其悲懷耳... 而傾心彼族者又誤
> 信西人寬待其藩屬，躍躍然欲趨而附之。則吾
> 書之足以儆醒之者，寧雲少哉？ (*Hei nu xu tian
> lu* 1)

Undoubtedly, it was this patriotic sentimentality that
helped the reception of Lin's translation very well; the
general and critical reviews focused their attentions on the
fate of Chinese as a race in the world. Lingshi's 1904 book
review was the typical reading of *Hei nu xu tian lu* 黑奴吁
天錄 (Black Slaves Sigh to the Heaven), the Chinese title
of Stowe's novel, at the time when the book was still well
received:

> We don't need to wait for the future to see the mis-
> fortunes of yellow people. The exclusion of Chinese
> laborers in America and the tortures of Chinese pe-
> ople in the West are recorded facts. The situation has
> no difference from that of black people, and may
> be even worse. How can you imagine our terrible

condition in the future? ... When I read *Hei nu xu tian lu*, I cried for our yellow race with the tears that I shed on black people, cried for the current situation of our yellow race in view of the miseries of the black suffered before. I wish every family of the yellow people would buy a copy of *Hei nu xu tian lu*. I wish everyone who has read *Hei nu xu tian lu* would cry out the sadness for his sons and daughters and shed hot tears for the heroes.

且黃人之禍，不必待諸將來，而美國之禁止華工，各國之虐待華人，已見諸事實，無異黑人，而較諸黑人而尤劇，則他日之苦況，其可設想耶？... 我讀《吁天錄》，以哭黑人之淚哭我黃人，以黑人以往之境，哭我黃人之現在，我欲黃人家家置一《吁天錄》。我願讀《吁天錄》者，人人發兒女之悲啼，灑英雄之熱淚。(*Chen* 131-32)

Because of the great popularity of the translated novel, Picha nü shi (Lady Beecher), a Chinese translation of the name of Harriet Beecher Stowe, became one of the three heroines who were worshipped by the Chinese revolutionaries and advocates for women's rights in the late nineteenth and early twentieth centuries.[*]

The political impetus behind Lin's translation is undeniable, but some incidents lead some readers to speculate on other unnamed or unspecified reasons about the start and the publication of this translation project. Both Lin Shu's preface and epilogue to the translation are widely

[*] *Situohuo nü shi* (Lady Stowe), Lin Shu's translation of Harriet Beecher Stowe, was known as the author of *Uncle Tom's Cabin*, while Picha nü shi was known as the author of *The May Flower* and became very popular after the publication of a Chinese translation of a Japanese biography of Harriet Beecher Stowe in 1902. For a long time, the Chinese readership didn't associate Situohuo nü shi with *Picha nü shi*, though they attributed to Picha nü shi the reputation of dissolving slavery in America with a novel. See Chapter 6 of Xia Xiaohong's book for a detailed discussion.

circulated: to credit their importance in Lin's translation theory and in the development of Chinese fiction, they are collected in many popular anthologies of Chinese literature and translation studies.* However, one fact is unknown even to many scholars who study Lin Shu: that is, in addition to Lin's preface, Wei Yi (1880-1932), his young collaborator, wrote a translator's preface too. This preface only found itself in the first edition of the translation, which was published by the Wei family in 1901, but disappeared from all the later editions. Wei's preface clarifies some aspects of this joint translation. We can get a clearer view of the translation process when juxtaposing Wei's preface with Lin's and his epilogue.

According to Lin, the original novel was obtained by Wei Yi from Qiushi shu yuan (Qiu shi College) in Hangzhou, one of the first established public postsecondary institutions in China. The translation proceeded in this way: when Wei Yi gave Lin his oral rendition of the story, Lin simultaneously phrased it in classical Chinese full of his style. During the sixty-six days of translating, the tragic conditions of the black slaves moved the two translators so much that they alternated translating while crying. Much of Lin's preface and epilogue was devoted to the introduction of the history of black slaves in America and the comparison of Chinese laborers in America and black slaves. What needs to be noted here is that it was this comparison that struck the hearts of Chinese readers. This translation established Lin Shu as not only a translator of a popular romance, but also a patriotic writer.

Wei Yi's preface, however, showed that it was Wei who read the novel first. He was moved immediately, and then

---

* They appear in Chen Pingyuan's *Er shi shi ji Zhongguo xiao shuo li lun zi liao* (Theoretical Documents of Twentieth Century Chinese Novel), A Ying's Wan Qing wen xue cong chao (Collections of Late Qing Literary Works), and *Lin Shu yan jiu zi liao* (Study Materials about Lin Shu). These are indispensable source books for scholars who study Late Qing literature.

introduced this book to Lin Shu. He also shared with Lin his understanding of the book: similarities between the miserable life of Chinese labors and that of black slaves, between the future of Chinese nation and the fate of black slaves. Unlike the reluctance shown in the first translation project, this time Lin Shu accepted Wei's suggestion of translating without any hesitation. What is more, he put his real name on the book, an action that he dared not take when publishing *Bali cha hua nü yi shi* 巴黎茶花女遺事 (The Legend of the Camellias of Paris Lady) in 1899, the translation of *La Dame aux caméllias* by Alexandre Dumas fils. Contrary to Lin Shu's claim that his motive to translate was politically charged, a consideration of literary fame surprisingly played an important role. By literary fame, I mean that Lin Shu earnestly and eagerly dissociated himself from the image of the translator of a foreign romance.[*]

Though the theme of *Uncle Tom's Cabin* fit the patriotic atmosphere in China, fiction as a genre was still regarded as vulgar and lowbred. Another motive for Lin was an attempt to domesticate the foreign work. He treated the original novel as a Chinese classic essay and analyzed it carefully. In the preface, Lin Shu noted that the way of writing demonstrated in *Uncle Tom's Cabin*, such as how to start, how to tell a story, and how to come to an ending, conformed to the canons of Chinese classics. He thus urged Chinese literati not to belittle Western literature. From then on, Lin Shu intentionally transformed foreign themes and structures into the ones acceptable to Chinese.

---

[*] Qian Zhongshu keenly noticed this psychological complex in Lin Shu when he recounted a personal talk with Chen Yuan, a late Qing poet and Lin Shu's friend. According to Chen, Lin Shu hated to be praised as translator and painter, though he deserved the two titles. But if his classic essays gained positive commentaries, he would be really happy. So Chen Yuan tried to teach Qian the proper way of reading Lin Shu's translation: read his translation in order to learn his classic writing skill. See Qian Zhongshu's *Lin Shu's Translations*.

If we take into consideration how Lin Shu managed his translation career, we will see clearly the constellation of Lin's motives to translate. In the preface to his *Bali cha hua nü yi shi* (*La Dame aux caméllias*), Lin Shu gave his readers a very brief account of how he started his first translation:

> Master of Dawning Studio came back from Paris and told Mr. Cold Red that all the novels in Paris were penned by famous writers. I asked him to give me some examples. Master said the works of Dumas père and *fils* were very popular in Paris and *La Dame aux caméllias* was a masterpiece by Dumas *fils*. Whenever he was free, Master recounted this novel to Mr. Cold Red and Mr. Cold Red wrote it down with his brush.

> 曉齋主任歸自巴黎，與冷紅生談巴黎小說家均出自名手。生請述之。主人因道，仲馬父子文字，于巴黎最知名，《茶花女馬克格尼爾遺事》尤為小仲馬極筆。暇輒述以授冷紅生，冷紅生涉筆記之。(*Bali cha hua nü yi shi* 1)

In this passage, Master of Dawning Studio is Lin Shu's friend and first collaborator Wang Shouchang, while Mr. Cold Red is Lin Shu himself. Though it was not clear who first came up with the idea of translating *La Dame aux caméllias*, the curiosity for newness and foreign literature played an important role in Lin's decision. His great interest in foreign literature also suggested that he should not have completely been passive in this project.

In *Huasuiren sheng an zhi yi* 花隨人聖盦摭憶 [Recollections from Huasuiren Cloister], Huang Jun (b. 1888) recorded this story from another perspective that suggested a different role of Lin Shu in translating:

> When Wei Han was in charge of the Engineering Office of the Fuzhou Shipyard, he was fooling around

with Lin Shu. One day he told Lin that French novels were very good and asked him to translate some, but Lin declined with the excuse of his incompetence. After Wei entreated him many times, Lin replied: "If you treat me to a trip to Stoned-drum Mountain, I will do it." Wei generously promised, and hired a ship and went on the trip with Wang Shouchang. Wei forced Wang to recount the story of *La Dame aux caméllias* ... After the book was published, the public was surprised and excited. Lin also felt very happy.

魏季渚（瀚）主马江船政工程处，与畏庐狎；一日告以法国小说甚佳，欲使译之，畏庐谢不能。再三强，乃曰："须请我游石鼓山乃可。"季渚慨诺，买舟载王子仁同往，强使口授《茶花女》... 书出而众哗悦，林亦欣欣。
(*Huang* 40)

This version of story gives Wei Han, Lin's and Wang's close friend and classmate, all the credit for introducing the source text, sponsoring the translation, and initiating the translation project. Wei Han functioned as a sponsor in that he not only sponsored a trip for the two translators, but also convinced Lin to work and organized Lin and Wang together to finish the translation. It is worth noting that such outings are favorite ways for Chinese writers to spend their leisure time, because nature provides them with inspirations for creation.

The most sensational but plausible description came from Qian Jibo's discussion of Lin Shu's classical verse in his *Xian dai Zhongguo wen xue shi* 現代中國文學史 (History of Modern Chinese Literature). Qian writes:

Lin Shu lost his wife. He always felt sorrow and showed no sign of happiness. So [Wang] Shouchang spoke to him: "May I ask you to translate a book with me? In so doing, you could disperse your loneliness

and I could introduce a famous book into China. This
is better than to sit face to face with sadness!" Then
the two together translated *La Dame aux caméllias* by
Dumas *père* [sic] and published it. The countrymen
were shocked by this unknown genre and tens of
thousands copies were sold.

> 紓喪其婦，牢愁寡歡！壽昌因語之曰："吾
> 請與子譯一書，子可以破岑寂；吾亦得以　介
> 紹一名著於中國，不勝於蹙額對坐耶！"遂與
> 同譯法國大仲馬《茶花女遺事》行世，國人詫
> 所未見，不脛走萬本！ (*Qian* 17)

In this case, translation served as no more than an an-
tidepressant for Lin Shu, while Wang Shouchang placed
high expectation and great ambition on this translation.

These three versions are more and less contradictory, but
in fact they could be woven together to reveal the truth behind Lin's first translation project. Admittedly, Lin Shu had
the idea of translating foreign books to enlighten Chinese
people long before he really started one. In the preface to
the *Translation Magazine*, a magazine set up by Lin Shu in
1901 to "translate comprehensively Western and Japanese
books for the Chinese literati's good," Lin Shu disclosed
the fact that he had asked Wei Yi, Wang Shouchang and
even a Frenchman to translate biographies of Napoleon
and Bismarck. The plan failed because of the difficulty
of the task and the unavailability of the translators (*Chen*
42). It is reasonable to argue that Lin Shu's unwillingness
to translate a foreign novel like *La Dame aux caméllias* lies
in political and aesthetic reservations. Politically, translating a love romance can hardly substantiate Lin's rather
pragmatic view of translation as an educational means.
Aesthetically, fiction was a low form in the eyes of Chinese
literati. Translating a foreign novel couldn't do anything
good for Lin Shu, but could tarnish his reputation as a
renowned classic essayist.

However, a traditional function of fiction granted Lin Shu a good excuse to translate *La Dame aux caméllias*. To traditional Chinese literati, writing a novel is acceptable when it is for pleasure. The loss of a wife gave Lin Shu a good reason to spare himself from serious writing. Though traditional Chinese literati have a long history of giving themselves pen names or sobriquets for various reasons, the reason that both Lin Shu and Wang Shouchang did not leave their real names on the book was that this was the customary action when writing a novel for fun. Thinking this way, it becomes understandable that Lin Shu's attitudes towards translating *La Dame aux caméllias* were ambivalent.

Lin Shu's different motives for translating his first two books reveal an entrenched cultural logic that governs Chinese literary writings. There exist two interpretations of the end of literature from the very beginning of Chinese culture: that poetry speaks of intentions and that poetry speaks of feelings. According to the classical Chinese text *Shang Shu* (The Book of History), a collection of the historical literature dating back at least to the second century BCE, the first statement is made by the legendary king Shun when he discusses his understandings of arts with his musical official Kui:

> The king said: Kui, I order you to preside over music and educate our sons of noble families, so that they become straightforward and gentle, congenial and dignified, strong and merciful, and simple and moderate. Poetry speaks of the intentions; singing prolongs the utterances. The notes accord with the utterances, and are harmonized by the pitch tubes. The eight kinds of musical instruments attain to harmony and do not interfere with one another. Spirits and man are thereby brought into harmony.

帝曰：夔！命汝典樂，教胄子，直而溫，
寬而慄，剛而無虐，簡而無傲。詩言志，歌永
言，聲依永，律和聲。八音克諧，無相奪倫，
神人以和。(*Ruan* 131)

Quite different from the modern understanding of intention as someone's plan, purpose, and goal, the Chinese sage casts it with ritualistic and sociopolitical connotations. Because the Confucian scholars were primarily interested in the moral implications of history, they started a significant reformulation of the concept in a moralistic and didactic direction in the Han dynasty (206 BCE–220 AD). The reinterpretation appears first in the "Preface to the Mao version of *The Book of Songs*," the "most authoritative statement on the nature and function of poetry in traditional China" (*Owen* 37). Poetry is conceived not as the creative practice of an individual poet but as a general human activity of social and political consequences. Poets write with the purpose of exposing social abuses. As a result, poetry serves as a means for the ruler to learn social reality and educate his subjects. As modern Chinese poet and scholar Zhu Zhiqing (1898-1948) succinctly points out, the intention in question "cannot be separated from the *li*, or propriety, nor from the political affairs and moral education" (9).

The interpretation of poetry as an expression of personal feelings first began to take root in the "Preface to *The Book of Songs*," side by side with a moralistic statement.

> Poetry is where the heart's wishes go. What lies in the heart is "wish"; when expressed in words, it is "poetry". When an emotion stirs within one, one expresses it in words; finding this inadequate, one sighs over it; not content with this, one sings it in poetry; still not satisfied, one unconsciously dances with one's hands and feet.

詩者，志之所之也，在心為志，發言為詩。
情動于中而形於言，言之不足，故嗟歎之，嗟
歎之不足故永歌之，永歌之不足，不知手之舞
之，足之蹈之也。(*Ruan* 261)

Devoid of explicit social and moral meanings, emotion
is appreciated solely for its aesthetic value. This idea of
poetry had been favored by Taoist writers ever since the
great master Zhuangzi and graduately came to dominate
Chinese literary thought. Along the way, certain emotions
have become the constant and conventional themes in
Chinese literature. No one who has read any amount of
Chinese poetry can fail to notice the quantity and quality of literary works on sorrow for the loss of a wife. As
a matter of fact, Sorrow Poetry became a special literary
term to designate those poems that express the writer's
sorrow for the death of his wife or concubine. We can find
this type of poem in *Shi jing* (The Book of Songs), the earliest anthology of poems in China.[*] Literary creation is an
effective way to diminish great sorrow for Chinese writers,
as Lin Shu's case demonstrates once again.

It would be a mistake to think that the two different interpretations of literature are held by two different circles
of writers. In fact, the gap between the two kinds of literature is not unbridgeable. The history of Chinese literature
always tells an interesting story: when a writer begins his
political career or is in the ascendancy, he tends to speak
of his political intentions in his writings; when he faces a
huge difficulty in his career and his political intentions are
frustrated, his writings are most likely to express his feelings of nostalgia, leisure, sorrow and the like. This kind of
complementary psychological mechanism enables Chinese
writers to write under different circumstances.

---

[*]   There are three poems what can be put under this rubric: Yanyan and
Lüyi (Green Clothes) of Songs of Bei, and Weinan (South of the Wei river)
of Songs of Qin.

Lin Shu's first two translation projects demonstrate perfectly this mechanism. As I discussed before, there were three versions of how Lin Shu started to translate *La Dame aux caméllias*. Curiosity, leisure and sadness are the essential elements in all three stories. It is quite likely that it was not just one feeling that motivated Lin Shu to translate a sad love story from the West; the translation actually speaks of Lin Shu's complex feelings.

At the time when Lin Shu worked on translating *Uncle Tom's Cabin*, he had just taken a teaching position at the Grand Imperial College in Beijing. Coming from a provincial city, Lin Shu was stimulated immediately by the cultural and political atmosphere in the capital. Besides teaching, he spent a lot of time socializing, which was how he got to know his young collaborator Wei Yi. At about the same time, Yan Fu spelled out his political intentions in a series of newspaper editorials motivated by the national crisis. Unlike him, Lin Shu spoke of his political intentions in a novel about slavery in America.

It is not my purpose to argue here that an intrinsic cultural logic controls Lin Shu's literary activities. Rather, I intend to illustrate Lin Shu as an anomaly in translation history by reading him against the tradition that cultivates him and by showing his intervention into the tradition. In his seminal paper "The task of the Translator," Walter Benjamin defines the task of the translator as "finding that intended effect upon the language into which he is translating which produces in it the echo of the original" (76). While Benjamin's "intended effect" carries an implication of a mythical philosophy of language, Lin Shu's Chinese translation of *Uncle Tom's Cabin* echoed the original more in terms of his political intentions and aspirations.

Translational Methodology

When introduced to the general readership, Lin Shu is often labeled a famous translator who knows no foreign languages. The reception to this label varies from one extreme to another. Surprise notwithstanding, some acclaim with pride the uniqueness of Lin Shu's mode of operation: "Lin Shu's way of translating is not only unique in Chinese translation history, but also unique in the translation history of the world" (*Xie* 71). This belief has not been seriously challenged until recently. As a matter of fact, team translation has dominated the long translation history of China and Lin Shu was actually among the last translators who worked in this collaborative tradition.

On the other extreme of the evaluation spectrum, others deny Lin Shu the title of translator. I mentioned before that Robert Compton doesn't consider Lin Shu as a translator "in the strictest sense of the word". This stance is based on the assumption that a translator be at least bilingual. This assumption makes sense, because on the front page of the translation of *Uncle Tom's Cabin*, the credit line goes as follows: "Recorded by Lin Shu and orally narrated by Wei Yi." No word referring to translation was used. But if Lin Shu is to be excluded from the translators' club, we will face a huge legacy for which we cannot account. André Lefevere saves us from the predicament by teaching us that translation can be regarded as a form of rewriting under the influence of cultural, social and political constraints in a society. The task of rewriting is to adapt the original work "to a different audience, with the intention of influencing the way in which that audience reads the work" (150). Judged by this norm, Lin Shu's endeavors indisputably fall under the category of translation.

To better understand the contribution of Lin Shu's team translations, we need to situate him in the translation history of China to figure out what changes he has brought in the translational paradigm.

With more and more studies on the translation history of China, it becomes more evident that teamwork represents the predominant form of translating activities in imperial China. However, it is still less known that team translation takes on different forms in different times at different places. As introduced before, the translating of Buddhist sutras into Chinese started as early as the first century of the Common Era. Changes in language efficiency, patronage, literary trends, and readership resulted in some significant changes in team translation. For an in-depth analysis, I categorize four types of team translation: Christian missionary translation, Buddhist translation, brush-up translation and classroom translation. Of the four types, the first two comprise the majority of team translations while the last two serve as interesting examples to expand our understanding of the translator. I will also discuss the different roles of collaborators and their implications to the outcome. I do not intend to give a historical account of team translation in China. Rather, I try to provide some models of how team translation worked according to their translation practices.

Generally speaking, a Christian missionary translation, which characterized late Ming and early Qing translations, is the result of joint work by two people: a Christian missionary and his Chinese assistant. The Christian missionary is knowledgeable about both the text's source language and Chinese, while the Chinese assistant is well versed in Chinese but doesn't know the source language. The translation operates like this: the Christian missionary orally translates the text into Chinese with his broken or adequate Chinese, while the Chinese assistant renders this oral version into written, and ideally literary, form. Depending on the nature and complexity of the text, the Christian missionary translator may or may not check the written version of the translation. But in the translating process, there would be varying degree of consultation and clarification between the two collaborators.

The translation of *Euclidis elementorum* is an example of this translation mode. The mastermind of this translation project was Matteo Ricci (1552-1610), arguably the most well-known Jesuit missionary in China. Matteo Ricci won his fame not only by his successful establishment of the first Catholic church in the empire's Capital, but also by his translations of Chinese classics into Latin and those of Western science books into Chinese. Lacking knowledge of the Chinese language, his predecessors had failed to spread the faith in China. Harboring his religious agenda, he started to learn Chinese language and culture. Translating Western science books with his Chinese friends was his way to please traditional Confucian literati and officials. To satisfy their great interest in science, Matteo Ricci decided to translate Euclid's Elements. Lacking confidence in his Chinese, especially his written Chinese, he invited Xu Guangqi (1562-1633) to work with him. Knowing no foreign languages, Xu was a *xiucai*, the equivalent of a person with bachelor's degree, and was good at writing. According to Matteo Ricci's preface to the book, he did his translation orally while Xu did a written version. The two frequently checked with one another for accurate meanings of the original and the best choice of the Chinese equivalent. The final version was finished after three drafts. In this case, Matteo Ricci had absolute authority over the original and also contributed a lot to the Chinese translation. The translation was attributed thus: orally delivered by Matteo Ricci, translated in writing by Xu Guangqi. The monolingual Xu was credited as translator, but his role in the project involved working only in the (written) Chinese. The difficulties Matteo Ricci and Xu Guangqi met in their translation showed that the quality of a Christian missionary translation depended on the closeness of the collaboration.

Federico Masini has brought to our attention a language issue regarding Matteo Ricci's Chinese. Since Matteo Ricci came to mainland China through Macao, his first linguistic contacts with China were likely with southern dialects. But his knowledge of the linguistic situation in China was amazingly correct: "With all this variety of languages, there is one which is called *guanhua* which is the legal language, used in hearings and courts; it is easily learnt in every province simply by using it and even children and women have sufficient familiarity with it" (*Masini* 6). The Chinese language Matteo Ricci learned was the *guanhua*, an oral language spoken by functionaries. This information matters to our topic in that it explains more about Xu Guangqi's role in the translation. A native of Shanghai, Xu communicated with Matteo Ricci through *guanhua* while he himself also spoke another dialect. But in translating, his job was to transform Matteo Ricci's *guanhua* rendition into classical Chinese.

In ancient China, the collaboration of two or more translators was also an integral part of the process of Buddhist translation. By Buddhist translation, I mean the normal process of the translation of a Buddhist text into Chinese in the Sui and Tang dynasties, when Buddhism gained high popularity in China and received financial and political support from the government. Owing to his erudite knowledge on the subject, a monk from India or Central Asia is positioned to preside over the translation of a classic Buddhist scripture. Unfortunately, the monk does not speak Chinese. One or more Chinese who know both Chinese and the monk's language are assigned to act as the monk's interpreter. More often than not, some other Chinese assistants will take up such duties as transcribing, copying, polishing, and editing. Depending on the scale of the translation project, the number of these Chinese participants will vary from several to hundreds. The translation team is well-organized and everyone is given a title. According to Shi Zanning (919-1001), the titles in Tang dynasty include: (1) *yizhu* 譯主 (chief of translation); (2) *zhengyi* 證義 (verifier of the meaning of the written Chinese); (3) *zhengfanben* 證梵本 (verifier of the meaning in the Sanskrit text); (4) *duoyu* 度語 (translator who recited the foreign text and translated it into Chinese); (5) *bishou* 筆受 (scribe who wrote the translation down in Chinese); (6) *canyi* 參譯 (proofreader); (7) *kanding* 刊定 (corrector of the Chinese characters) and (8) *runwen* 潤文 (polisher of style).

Kumarajiva (343?-413?) was one of the most prolific monk translators in Chinese history. He and his collaborators produced a series of translations, including the *Amitabha Sutra*, basic text of the Pure Land school in China, *Perfection of Wisdom* in 25,000 lines, *Treatise on the Great Perfection of Wisdom*, and the two important Mahayana scriptures, *Lotus of the Good Law* and *Sutra Spoken by Vimalakirti* (*Ma* 37). Trained in both Theravada and Mahayana classics from his early age, Kumarajiva earned his fame as an erudite at only nineteen years of age. Through an extended and complicated process, Kumarajiva finally settled down in Chang'an in 401, a center bustling with Buddhist activities, where he set up a translation workshop to retranslate the most influential of the Mahayana scriptures and produce definitive editions with authoritative interpretations. Having spent more than 18 years in China before coming to Chang'an, Kumarajiva gained a wonderful knowledge of Chinese language and culture. However, as *yizhu* (chief of translation), he depended on numerous assistants of his in translating sutras, since besides oral translation, he had to explicate the thrust of the text to an audience of more than 1,000 followers. This is not suggesting that he played little part in translation. In addition to expounding the content, Kumarajiva appreciated very much the literary nature of the sutras. He felt very disappointed with previous translations in that they did not replicate the beauty of language and rhetoric in the original. To pursue literary beauty, he considered editing the original acceptable and necessary in translation. His ideas about translation had great impact on the translation practices of his assistants. Buddhist translation took a turn ever since from favoring literal translation to favoring free translation.

However, we cannot take Kumarajiva's free translation as irresponsible dealings with the original. Seng Rui, one of his famous pupils, recalled the process of translating the *Treatise on the Great Perfection of Wisdom*: "[Kumarajiva] held the original in his hands ... Chinese translation came out from his mouth. If there existed two interpretations, all attendants argued about the real meaning of the text. ... Working together with more than five hundred old friends and monks, they tried to exhaust the meaning of the original and deliberated on the wording of translation, and then the final translation was written down" (*Luo* 60). We can see from this record that Kumarajiva was extremely serious about the translation and worked closely with his collaborators. Kumarajiva stands as some sort of exception to the Buddhist translation mode.

"Brush-up" translation refers to a special translation mode that is recognized as translation very recently. In brush-up translation, a Chinese man of letters with little or no knowledge of the source language decides that a better version of the text needs to be done, since none of previous translations are felt adequate by comparison, mostly in terms of their stylistic features. He then produces a new translation by editing previous versions and making stylistic changes. Xie Lingyun's version of the *Mahaparinirvana sutra* serves as a good example to this method. Before Xie

Lingyun (385-433) worked with his friend monks Huiguan and Huiyan on a new translation of the *Mahaparinirvana sutra*, there had existed two previous versions: one by Dharmaraksa of Central Asia, the other by the Chinese monk Faxian. As one of the foremost poets of his era and a devout Buddhist, Lin was very disappointed with the crudeness and plainness of the existing translations. Knowing nothing about the source language, Xie and his collaborators simply used Dharmaraksa's translation as a basis and did some editing and polishing to make their translation (*Qu* 38-42).

In fact, the duties of Xie Lingyun might only be called editing. However, some Chinese scholars give him the title of translator. Jiang Shuzhuo justifies his claim in the name of re-evaluation: "China's circles have always been prejudiced against translation and translators. ... Even the translation work of such a great poet and great translator as Xie Lingyun has been ignored by literary historians" (22). In his 1992 book *Translation, Rewriting and the Manipulation of Literary Fame*, Andre Lefevere pointed out that rewriting includes anthologies, histories of literature, works of literary criticism, and editions, as well as children's versions of texts, films, and cartoons. Like translations, all these types rework source texts in one way or another. Rewriting is subject to manipulation since it is influenced by certain linguistic, ideological and poetic factors. In this case, we see clearly double manipulations at work: Xie Lingyun manipulates the two previous translations and critics like Jiang Shuzhuo manipulate Xie's case to promote the position of translation and translators. Though brush-up translation can be covered by translation studies, it can only represent a small part of translations.

Classroom translation is the product of the modernization of the traditional education system. A foreigner is offered a teaching job in a language or technical school.

Chinese students are enrolled to learn a foreign language and modern sciences and technologies. As a training method, translating a foreign book is used by the Western teacher to check the students' command of the foreign language. Students are asked to translate part of a book, usually a science book, and the teacher corrects the draft translations and makes the final version. This was once a common teaching practice In *Tong wen guan* (Interpreters' College) and other government-sponsored translation institutions in the late Qing era, such as the translation bureau affiliated Jiangnan Shipyard.

Lin Shu's collaboration with Wei Yi on *Uncle Tom's Cabin* is an obvious example of the Christian missionary translation mode. Though the information about the process of translation in Lin Shu's preface is very limited, we can still have a sense of how the translation proceeded. The translation took them sixty-six days. When translating, Wei Yi gave Lin his oral translation while Lin simultaneously phrased it in classical Chinese. As a follower of the Tongcheng School, a mid-Qing literary circle which stressed the elucidation of the article's purpose and favored concise and natural writing, Lin's classical Chinese is very stylish. There's no evidence suggesting Wei checked Lin's translation. On the occasion of another translation project, a similar process was recorded. In the preface to his version of Dickens's *Old Curiosity Shop*, Lin Shu recalled, "I listened with my ears and followed [the oral narration] with my hand. When the voice stopped, so did my brush. Working a mere four hours a day, we could get 6,000 words done" (*xiao nü nai'er zhuan* 1).

Lin's accounts have shown us a picture in which he was the dominant party in the collaboration. A contrary report comes from the other side of the collaboration. To celebrate the one-hundredth anniversary of the publication of *Uncle Tom's Cabin*, Wei Yi's daughter Wei Weiyi published a new edition of all the translations that were done by Lin Shu and Wei Yi. In the postscript, she described the working relation between Lin Shu and her father:

> Lin was the great master of the Tongcheng School and his Chinese was strong. But he didn't know any foreign language and depended solely on my father's oral narration. He didn't quite understand that the translation must be faithful to the original and making changes to the original isn't allowed. Since he always tried to add in his ideas [in the translation], my father was often in conflict with him. Mr. Lin followed my father's opinion all the time and only documented his in the book's margins. (100)

There must be some truth in this recollection about Wei Yi's authority over the original and Lin Shu's translation. It also explains why Lin Shu made his collaborators accountable for errors in the translations. History, however, seemed to tell another story. After he worked with Wei Yi, Lin Shu continued to gain great fame as the translator of a number of popular western novels. Throughout his life, Lin Shu worked with more than twenty collaborators, most of whom were forgotten by the reader. For those who still appear in the history textbooks, their names are remembered only in association with Lin Shu. Wei Yi is one. Wei Yi translated some novels by himself at the time when translated Western novels were still in fashion, but all of them turned out to be a commercial failure. If Wei Yi played a major role in his collaboration with Lin Shu, how can we explain the obscurity of his fame and of his own translations? Lin Shu is certainly a special case in team translation.

There is another phenomenon worth a moment to ponder. As I have shown above, team translation has dominated translation history in China for more than one thousand years. But after Lin Shu, this format of translating came to an end, with only a short period of revival after the founding of the People's Republic of China. No matter what caused the disappearance of Wei Yi's "Translator's Preface" from the book, it marked symbolically the death of team translation in China. If the bilingual translator is deprived of the right to voice his opinion on translation, collaboration with a monolingual translator becomes unnecessary. The more fame the monolingual translator earns, the greater urgency of the bilingual translator to break up with his partner. It may be too harsh to say Lin Shu is the closer of team translation. The rapid increase in the number of the bilingual Chinese is another important factor. However, the literary fame and the commercial success Lin Shu won as/for translator definitely gave a heavy blow to team translation. The way Lin Shu broke team translation demonstrates that his practice was an anomaly in the translation history of China.

Translational Techniques

In this section, I will take a close look at a small portion of Lin Shu's translation of *Uncle Tom's Cabin*. The common method used to study a translation text is of strong impressionistic character: researchers tend to summarize certain features of the translation which are demonstrated by examples of some isolated words or sentences in the text. This method can hardly provide the reader with a full picture of the whole translation project. Instead of giving some sporadic examples in Lin Shu's translation, I examine parts of his translation of considerable length. The first part of Chapter XIIIV is chosen for the close reading. In the following, I juxtapose the original with the translation to help identify Lin Shu's mistranslations. The reason I do this isn't that I wish to ridicule his mistakes and incompetence as translator. Rather, I want the answers to questions such as: What kinds of changes did Lin make? Why did he make these changes? Was his translation faithful to the original?

~~English:~~ Omission English: Shift [...]: Paraphrase (...): Addition

CHAPTER XVIII

第十八章

Miss Ophelia's Experiences and Opinions

~~Our friend~~ Tom, in his own ~~simple~~ musings, often compared his more fortunate lot, in the bondage into which he was cast, with that of [Joseph in Egypt]; and, in fact, as time went on, and he developed more and more under the eye of his master, the strength of the parallel increased.

湯姆自隸聖格來家，雖操作不以為苦，以奴籍中受笞撻者多於我也。久之，聖格來稔其性情，亦漸不以奴處之。

St. Clare was indolent and careless of money. Hitherto the providing and marketing had been principally done by Adolph, who was, ~~to the full,~~ as careless and extravagant ~~as his master; and, between them both, they~~ had carried on the dispersing process with great alacrity. [Accustomed, for many years,] to regard his master's property as his own care, Tom saw, with an uneasiness ~~he could scarcely repress,~~ the wasteful expenditure of the establishment; ~~and, in the quiet, indirect way which his class often acquire, would sometimes make his own suggestions.~~

聖格來之為人，佻撻無遠識，不審家人作苦。湯姆未至，凡會計出入，均阿道而夫司之。阿道而夫亦不心主人家事，以其資財任意揮霍。湯姆事主人忠，每於毫末之物，亦視為己產，（彌複珍惜。）滋不悅阿道而夫所為。

St. Clare at first employed him occasionally; ~~but, struck with his soundness of mind and good business capacity,~~ he confided in him more and more, till gradually all the marketing and providing for the family were intrusted to him. ~~"No, no, Adolph," he said, one day, as Adolph was deprecating the passing of power out of his hands; "let Tom alone. You only understand what you want; Tom understands cost and come to; and there may be some end to money, bye and bye if we don't let somebody do that."[22]~~

Trusted to an unlimited extent by a careless master, [who handed him a bill without looking at it, and pocketed the change without counting it,] Tom had every facility and temptation to dishonesty; and nothing but an impregnable simplicity of nature, ~~strengthened by Christian faith,~~ could have kept him from it. But, to that nature, the very unbounded trust reposed in him was bond and seal for the most scrupulous accuracy.

~~With Adolph the case had been different. Thoughtless and self-indulgent, and unrestrained by a master who found it easier to indulge than to regulate, he had fallen into an absolute confusion as to _meum tuum_ with regard to himself and his master,~~

聖格來微省其事，漸遷阿道而夫之愛愛揚姆，（繼而盡削阿道而夫之）權利，悉授湯姆矣。

聖格來既昧于出納，一任司會計者所為，人以為湯姆握利權，又重以主人之寵，可以因緣為奸利。而湯姆銜恩切，一不敢以欺主人。

54

which sometimes troubled even St. Clare. His own good sense taught him that such a training of his servants was unjust and dangerous. A sort of chronic remorse went with him everywhere, although not strong enough to make any decided change in his course; and this very remorse reacted again into indulgence. He passed lightly over the most serious faults, because he told himself that, if he had done his part, his dependents had not fallen into them.

Tom regarded his gay, airy, handsome young master with an odd mixture of fealty, reverence, and fatherly solicitude. That he never read the Bible; never went to church; that he jested and made free with any and every thing that came in the way of his wit; that he spent his Sunday down his cheeks.

"You poor, silly fool!" said St. Clare, [with tears in his own eyes.] "Get up, Tom. I'm not worth crying over."

But Tom wouldn't rise, and looked imploring.

"Well, I won't go to any more of their cursed nonsense, Tom," said St. Clare; "on my honor, I won't. I don't know why I haven't stopped long ago. I've always despised _it_, and myself for it,—so now, Tom, wipe up your eyes, and go about your

湯姆（語至此，）喉哽不能發聲，淚隨之落。

聖格來見狀，亦淚落如綫，趣湯姆起，曰："吾薄德，（恐不任爾為奴也。）"湯姆見聖格來未誓言改過事，仍長跽不起。

errands. ~~Come, come,"~~ he ad-
~~ded, "no blessings. I'm not so~~
~~wonderfully good, now," he said,~~
~~as he gently pushed Tom to the~~
~~door. "There, I'll pledge my ho-~~
~~nor to you, Tom, you don't see~~
~~me so again," he said; and Tom~~
~~went off,~~ wiping his eyes, [with
great satisfaction].

"I'll keep my faith with him,
too," <u>said St. Clare</u>, ~~as he closed~~
~~the door.~~

~~And St. Clare did so,—for~~
~~gross sensualism, in any form,~~
~~was not the peculiar temptation~~
~~of his nature.~~

聖格來會意，乃語之
曰：「吾此後更不與彼譙
矣。」

因出矢言，麾之使出。湯
姆（見主人知悔，）大悅，
（以手）拭其餘淚而去。

聖格來因自語曰：「吾今
日許湯姆，當必如其約。」

What strikes us most when we look at the comparison is the length of Lin Shu's translation. Lin made many omissions to the original. In literary translation, omission is a common practice, but the reason behind this strategy varies from translator to translator, including the needs of the target culture, the acceptance of readers, current social, political or historical conditions, or the verbosity and untranslatability of the original text.

The first omission we find is the chapter title. This may look strange since traditional Chinese novels also use the chapter title to recapture the basic plot of the chapter. In his translator's preface, Lin Shu tells the reader that the novel's structure meets the requirements of classics. For the Chinese readers who would be familiar with traditional Chinese novels, the fact that the foreign novel had chapter titles would fulfill their expectation that western and Chinese fictions have something in common. This is the impression Lin Shu wants his readers to have. It can also be argued that Lin Shu didn't include chapter titles because he was trying to achieve the effect of estrangement: Chinese readers will notice the difference between Chinese and western fiction. But this argument is in conflict with Lin Shu's Sinicization strategy suggested in the translator's preface. Whatever the reason was, the acceptance of readers played an important role when Lin Shu made his decision.

The longest omission consists of two passages that describe Tom's thinking about his master's personalities and hobbies. The author tries to reveal Tom's inner psychological activities to show us Tom's loyalty. Though this kind of psychological description is essential to character-building, it has nothing to do with the development of the story. Since traditional Chinese fiction took shape in the tradition of story-telling, plot matters much more than character to the Chinese reader. Lin Shu's decision to omit all the passages makes sense to the Chinese reader.

In the preface, Lin Shu makes two points about how to deal with religious materials in his translation. First, he finds that "the writer is an American, and Americans are devout Christians. Their talk is all bound up with religion." However, He and Wei Yi were not Christians. As translators, they had to convey the religious message nonetheless. So Lin Shu pleaded "for understanding from those who are enlightened and educated." Second, he wrote that "a considerable part of the novel is about matters relating to the church. Wei Yi has omitted the trivial details for the convenience of readers. It is hoped that the translators will not be castigated for these omissions." There were such examples in the passages I examine. In the first passage, the original "Joseph in Egypt" was not translated. This must be considered as a "trivial" detail and was omitted for the good of the readers. But Lin Shu does keep the message of Tom's referring to Bible. However, in the translation Lin Shu makes the quotation from the Bible sound like a phrase in a classical Chinese essay.

From these omissions, Lin Shu's motive of translating the novel is revealed as he states in the preface and postscript of his translation. As a reader when he "listened to" Wei Yi's oral narration, Lin Shu was very clear about what the target culture and readers would need, and as a translator, he was also clear about how to meet those needs.

Remarks

As Zheng Hailing points out, "After all Lin Shu was a veteran writer in the literary world of China; with the help of others, he actually made his translations basically close to the originals, and added the finishing touch or gilded refined gold, translating more than one hundred Western classical works" (34). Zheng refutes the claim of "unfaithfulness" in Lin Shu's translation by demonstrating that a kind of poetic equivalence in Lin Shu's translation is obtained by Sinicization. Sinicization was Lin Shu's common strategy when dealing with foreign customs and culture. In so doing, Lin Shu domesticated a translated text into a Chinese linguistic and literary style, so as to make it read like a Chinese one. At the price of the original, Sinicization gained huge popularity in the translations of early modern China and general acceptance of the Chinese reader. Lin Shu's choice of the Sinicization strategy was not only a poetic consideration, but also conditioned by his historical surroundings.

In the next chapter, I turn to the work of the distinguished translator Yan Fu. Among the first Qing literati to advocate political and social reforms, Yan Fu definitely took translation as a political weapon to influence Qing officials' attitude toward the West. Yan Fu shares with Lin Shu the same idea of translation as a didactic tool. However, the two great translators differ from each other in many regards. Unlike Lin who knows no foreign language, Yan Fu learned English when he was a teenager and studied at a British naval academy for more than two years. Yan's good command of English well prepared him as a translator. While Lin Shu is notorious for his free translation, Yan Fu wins a reputation as a careful and faithful translator. Compared with Lin Shu, Yan Fu cannot be regarded as a prolific translator; he translated only seven books over his life. Both translators made great efforts to learn to write classic essays of the Tongcheng style, the only style recognized by the literary elites. Both of them were finally accepted by leading literati and regarded as great classic essayists. But Lin Shu only translates literary works while Yan Fu's translations are social science books. These differences raise many questions regarding their translation strategies: how does language capacity contribute to the choice of title to be translated and translation method? Is Yan Fu's translation really literary to the original? What does "literary translation" mean to Yan Fu as he stresses fidelity most? Besides subject matter, what translation methods does Yan Fu use to execute his political agenda? Is marketability ever a factor in Yan Fu's translation career? Those questions will be addressed in the next chapter.

Chapter Two

CHINA IN A NEW GEOPOLITICAL MAP: YAN FU'S TRANSLATION OF **EVOLUTION AND ETHICS**

It is safe to assume that Yan Fu's 1898 translation of T. H. Huxley's *Evolution and Ethics* would have topped for about twenty years the national bestsellers chart, if there were one at his time. Numerous documents have recorded the book's extreme popularity and tremendous influence. Schoolteachers used his translation as a textbook and composition topic; quite a few youths changed their names to or named their babies with Chinese translations of terms such as "natural selection," "survival of the fittest," and "struggle for survival"; leading political and public opinion figures sang high praise for his fine translation. Kang Youwei (1858-1927), a famous Chinese scholar who played a pivotal role in late Qing intellectual scene, once wrote a poem to Yan Fu as a birthday present. One line goes, "Of all the translators of all time, Yan [Fu] and Lin [Shu] are the best" (*Kang* 1).* In his autobiography, Hu Shi (1891-1962),

---

*   Unfortunately, Kang's compliment received negative responses from both Yan Fu and Lin Shu. Yan Fu didn't seem to regard Lin as a translator.

the most important liberal philosopher in modern China, described vividly how he and his middle school classmates were fascinated by Yan Fu's translation. When he was going to study at Cornell University in 1910, he chose *Shi* as his first name that connotes "fit for survival" (*Hu* 24).

The popular recognition of the book sounds more unbelievable if one considers that Yan Fu translated it into a classical Chinese that was used only by literati. Though a great advocate of Yan Fu's evolutionist idea, Liang Qichao complained about the esoteric tendency in his translation: "In his style he is too concerned with profundity and elegance. He is firmly bent on copying the style of the pre-Ch'in period [the third century B. C. and earlier], and those who have not read many ancient books found his translations most difficult to comprehend" (*Schwartz* 93). However, Yan Fu's *Tian yan lun* (Evolution and Ethics)* won the hearts of young students and open-minded intellectuals. The reason lay partly in the proliferation of the idea of natural selection, an alarming idea that struck the hearts of Yan Fu's contemporaries at a time when the survival of the Qing court and the Chinese people was a matter for concern. The success of Yan Fu's translation also lay partly in the introduction of the new historical thinking that was embedded in Huxley's evolutionist ideas. Until Yan Fu's introduction of Darwinism, China had not produced any serious philosophical thinking that viewed history as a linear progress towards an ultimate goal. The worldview of traditional Chinese people had been shaped by the belief that time cycles and life reincarnates. Huxley

---

He reportedly said, "In the world, one cannot be called translator if he knows no foreign language." Lin Shu was not satisfied with Kang's poem because Kang put his name behind Yan Fu. Another reason could be that Lin Shu was so proud of his classical essays that he preferred to be called essayist.

* Yan Fu's Chinese title means literally "On Evolution": *tian* means "heaven, nature, god," *yan* "change, evolution", and *lun* "discussion, discourse."

provided Chinese people with a brand-new picture of the world and forced them to accept a new spatial and temporal framework. This framework triggered the birth of modernity in China and consequently the rise of Chinese nationalism.

Drawing on Walter Benjamin, Jacque Derrida, and Paul de Man, Tejaswini Niranjana has argued that there exists an inequality in translation between languages, and has linked Western translations of third world works to the rise and spread of Western nationalism and imperialism (*Niranjana* 119). Yan Fu's translation was obviously politically charged, but he did not interpret the difficulties he met in translation in a political fashion as Niranjana suggests. The three criteria of translation Yan Fu proposed, namely, accuracy, intelligibility, and elegance,* seemingly concern only language and style. Praised as the highest norms when it comes to judge a translation, Yan Fu's

---

* The earliest translation of this triad seemed to be made by Achilles Fang in his discussion of translating Chinese literature. (Fang, 1959:129) There exist many other translations of those terms by different scholars. Theo Hermans (2003) gives us a list of those translations:

xin	da	ya	
faithfulness	comprehensibility	elegance	C.Y. Hsiu 1973: 4
faithfulness	communicability	elegance	Hung & Pollard 1998: 371
faithfulness	expressiveness	elegance	Wang Nin 1996: 43
faithfulness	expressiveness	gracefulness	Liu Miqin 1995a: 3
trueness	intelligibility	elegancy	Huang Yushi 1995: 278
faithfulness	expressiveness	elegance	Ma Zuyi 1995: 382
faithfulness	comprehensibility	elegance	Gilbert Fong 1995: 582
faithfulness	comprehensibility	elegance of style	Elisabeth Sinn 1995: 441
fidelity	intelligibility	elegance	Wu Jingrong 1995: 529
faithfulness	intelligibility	elegance	Wang Zongyan 1995: 560
'to be faithful,	expressive	Elegant	Wang Zuolian 1995: 999
faithfulness	readability	refinement	Fan Shouyi 1994: 152
fidelity	fluency	elegance	Yuen Ren Chao
faithfulness	comprehensibility	elegance	Xing Lu 1998: 10
fidelity	clarity or comprehensibility	elegance	Venuti 1998: 182

criteria have dominated the Chinese discourse on translation for more than a century. However, controversies are still lingering over the definition, origin, and implication of these three simple words. I will give an account of the controversies in the next section.

xin 信, da 达, ya 雅

In "General Remarks on Translation," one of the three prefaces to *Tian yan lun* (Evolution and Ethics), Yan Fu laid out his ideas on translation in general and some issues involved translating Thomas Henry Huxley. At the very beginning of this preface, Yan Fu gives us his famous three-word norm for translation: "Translation has to accomplish three difficult things: accuracy, intelligibility, and elegance. For a translation to be faithful to the original is difficult enough, and yet if it is not intelligible, it is tantamount to having no translation. Hence intelligibility should also be required" (*Yan* 26). After he makes a comparison of the Chinese and English languages, he turns to ancient Chinese sages to elaborate his third criterion *ya* (elegance): "The *Book of Changes* says that rhetoric should uphold sincerity. Confucius says that intelligibility is all that matters in language. He adds that if one's language lacks elegance, it will not travel far. These three qualities are the right way to compose a good writing and the model of good translation too. Therefore, in addition to accuracy and intelligibility, elegance should be pursued" (*Yan* 26).

Lu Xun is the first scholar to mention the influence of Sanskrit translations on Yan Fu's translation theory. In a letter discussing translation issues, Lu Xun told his addressee Qu Qiubai (1899-1935), an early Chinese communist leader and a translator, that "in order to do translation, Yan Youlin [Yan Fu's public name] once checked the methods used in translating Sanskrit scriptures in the dynasties of Han, Wei, and Six Dynasties" (380). He also viewed all Yan Fu's translations as a "miniature of the history of translating Sanskrit scriptures from the Han to the Tang dynasty" (380). In the late Han dynasty, translators highly valued literal translation, a method Yan Fu did not follow. On the contrary, Yan Fu took translations in the Six Dynasties (220-589 A.D.) as his model since they were comprehensible and elegant. Tang dynasty (618-907 A.D.) translations placed accuracy as their first norm, which led to low comprehensibility. According to Lu Xun, Yan Fu's late translations were influenced by Tang translations and became hard to understand. Qian Zhongshu, an erudite Chinese scholar, gives us a very specific source and claims that Lin Shu's expectations of a good translation go way back to the Three Kingdom period (220-280 A.D.) (*Qian* 1239). In his study of ten Chinese classical books, he asserts that Yan Fu's three words can be located in Zhi Qian's preface to the Chinese translation of the Dhammapada. In the preface, Zhi Qian, a third-century translator who translated several Buddhist texts into Chinese, gives an account on his contention with another translator and their theoretical agreement on the basic principle for the translation of scripture:

> Sanskrit and Chinese are completely different languages. It is said that Sanskrit books are from Heaven. Different terms and things make it not easy to communicate [between the two languages]. ... Notwithstanding a perfect command of Sanskrit, Zhu Jiangyan [the translator of the *Dhammapada*] was rather weak in clear Chinese, which led him to a rather blunt literal translation as the result of direct borrowing or transliteration. I fear his translation isn't elegant. ... All my colleagues said: Laozi taught us "beautiful words are not faithful, faithful words not beautiful." Confucius also taught us "Writing cannot express what is said, speech cannot express what is in the mind." In rendering Buddhist instructions, what

should be accorded is their original meaning free
from any polish.

天竺言語與漢異音，云其書為天書，語為
天語。名物不同，傳實不易...將炎雖善天竺
語，未備曉漢。其所傳言或得胡語，或以義
出音，近於質直。僕初嫌其辭不雅...座中
咸曰：“老氏稱，美言不信，信言不美。仲
尼亦云，書不盡言，言不盡意。明聖人意深
邃無極。今傳胡義，實宜經達。(*Taisho   shinshu
Daizokyo* 147)

The principle of "literal adherence to the original text"
was established as the first Chinese theorizing on translation and prevailed in translating Sanskrit scriptures for
more than two hundred years. Qian Zhongshu correctly
pointed out a historical fact, namely that accuracy, intelligibility, and elegance were the topics of a polemic on translation almost two thousand years before Yan Fu's preface.
The difference between the two attempts at a general
principle of translation is that Zhi Qian and Yan Fu had
different views on the relation of the three requirements;
therefore, they adopted different approaches in translating. Zhi Qian was convinced that the original meaning
of Buddhist masters matters more than intelligibility and
literary qualities were obstacles to the understanding of
meaning. Though based on the instructions of two great
Chinese thinkers, Zhi Qian's narrow interpretation of *ya*
(elegance) as "literary polishing" rendered a lot of translations problematic. Qian Zhongshu critiques Zhi Qi for not
understanding a basic traditional philosophical idea, that
is, to be faithful one has to forget the words themselves in
order to catch the meaning in/of them.

On the contrary, Yan Fu much values aesthetic and stylistic considerations. In his opinion, the problem of *ya* in
translation appears first as a language problem: What kind

of language does one use to translate? As I mentioned in the last chapter, traditional Chinese writers used a certain kind of written language to compose poetry and essays, the only two literary genres recognized as high literature. This written language is termed wenyan (classical Chinese), literally meaning literary language. Though with some exceptions, works of fiction were mainly written in a spoken Chinese language called *baihua* (vernacular language), literally meaning plain language. The hierarchy between classical and vernacular Chinese remained unchanged until the Mandarin movement in the 1920s standardized Chinese language and formed the national language (See Masini, 1993). Like Lin Shu, Yan Fu decided to conduct his translation in classical Chinese. But unlike Lin Shu, Yan Fu valued the Chinese language used in pre-Han classics. The pre-Han period refers to dynasties of Xia (2100-1800 B.C), Shang (c. 1700-1027 BCE), Zhou (1027-221 BCE) and Qin (221-206 BCE). While some scholars attribute Yan Fu's pre-Han style translation to his conservative ideology, more sympathetic reviews try to historicize Yan Fu's choice. Lu Xun, a great admirer of Yan Fu and fervent believer of evolutionism, contends that Yan Fu's intention was to seek approval from literary authorities to elevate the status of translation:

Why did he [Yan Fu] play this trick of [using pre-Han classical Chinese]? The answer is: The returned students at that time hadn't gained the high reputation they have now. The general public thought Westerners were only good at making machineries, especially alarm clocks; as a result, the returned students couldn't be categorized as *shi* (literati) because their only expertise was to speak the devil's languages. In view of this, he chose the pre-Han classical style and Wu Ruilun [a leading literary critic and essayist with pre-Han style] was willing to write him a preface. Since Wu's preface, other requests for translation came continuously.

> 那么，他为什么要干这一手把戏呢？答案是：那时的留学生没有现在那么阔气，社会上大抵以为西洋人只会做机器——尤其是自鸣钟——留学生只会讲鬼子话，所以算不了"士"人的。因此他便来铿锵一下子，铿锵得吴汝纶也肯给他作序，这一序，别的生意也就源源而来了。(381)

Beside the reason Lun Xun pointed out, Yan Fu's choice was not without aesthetic considerations. Though many pre-Han classics are still in curricula in China, the meaning and syntax of those classics became hard to access for traditional Chinese literati. Yan Fu obviously had a different thought in this regard. In his "General Remarks on Translation," Yan Fu defended his use of classical Chinese: "In using the syntax and style of the pre-Han period one actually facilitates the comprehensibility of the profound principles and subtle thoughts whereas in using the modern vernacular one finds it difficult to make things comprehensible" (1322). One should bear in mind that the target readers in Yan Fu's mind must have been the highly educated gentry-literati, because Yan Fu made it clear that he was not in pursuit of the effect that his translation would "travel far." Instead, he wanted his translation to be confined in those who could appreciate both the content and the style of his translation:

> My translation has received many criticisms for its obscure language and crude style. Actually I did this intentionally for comprehensibility. And the content of the book is mainly about practical knowledges such as logic, mathematics and science as well as astronomy. If a reader is not familiar with these studies,

even if he is of the same nationality and speaks the same language as the author, he won't be able to comprehend much, far less by reading a translation.

不佞此譯，頗貽艱深文陋之譏，實則刻意求顯，不過如是。又原書論說，多本名數格致，及一切疇人之學，倘於之數者屢未問津，雖作者同國之人，言語相通，仍多未喻，矧夫出以重譯也耶！(1322)

This paragraph indicates that: firstly, Yan Fu was keenly aware of his readership and consciously chose his translation strategies. When Lin Shu translated *Uncle Tom's Cabin*, he appealed to a general but imaginative Chinese people. When he translated *Evolution and Ethics*, Yan Fu, however, targeted a small portion of Chinese literati who traditionally exerted great influence on policy-making and public opinion. Secondly, his interpretation of ya involved an attempt at matching the style of the source text. Yan Fu's refutation suggests that his "obscure language and crude style" reflects the profoundness of the original. In modern terminology, both Lin Shu and Yan Fu are target-oriented. Since Lin Shu was not able to read the original, he could only replicate the "spirit" of the source text with the help of his extraordinary literary imagination. On the other hand, Yan Fu's language capability enables him to do more. To assure his readers of the accuracy of his translation, Yan Fu claims his translation "does not follow the exact order of words and sentences of the original text, but reorganizes and elaborates. However, it does not deviate from the original ideas" (1321). Yan Fu's efforts to replicate the idea and style of the original remind us of John Dryden's theory. In his preface to his translation of Virgil's *Aeneid*, Dryden laid out his translation method as "to keep as near my author as I could, without losing all his graces, the most eminent of which are in the beauty of his works" (*Munday* 42). Finally, the requirement of *ya* is not so much a concern of literary and aesthetic qualities as a means to facilitate the comprehensibility of a translation. Lin Shu's logic sounds absurd, because, as Liang Qichao complained, "his translation is so esoteric and antiquated resulting from his intentional imitation of pre-Han style, that only those who are knowledgeable in classics can understand" (*zhuanji* v.10 112). But since the elite literati "who are knowledgeable in classics" were actually Yan Fu's target readers, Yan Fu's pursuit of *ya* as both an aesthetic quality as well as a comprehensibility consideration did improve the acceptance of his translation. Eugene Eoyang succinctly summarizes, "In a sense, both Yen Fu and Lin Shu, each in their way, 'sinicized' the Western works they translated: they incorporated them into the Chinese tradition, and they sought in them values and beauties that the elite Chinese reader would recognize" (*Eoyang* 165-166).

In addition to the Chinese influences, a foreign source of Yan Fu's principles of translation has also been proposed by some scholars. Wu Jianguang first mentioned an unspecified foreign source of Yan Fu's translation theory. According to Wu Lifu, Wu's son and a modern Chinese translator, the unspecified foreign source was the Scottish translator Alexander Fraser Tytler (See Luo 458-462).* Qian Zhongshu also expressed the same idea in a private letter, which has not yet been published (See Hermans 20-21). In 1791, Tytler published his famous book *Essays on the Principles of Translation*, "the first systematic theoretical volume on translation" (*Bassnett* 391). Opposed to the

---

* Wu Guangjian's opinion about this issue is worth consideration because of his relationship with Yan Fu. Wu (1866-1943) was one of the first students enrolled in the Northern Sea Naval Academy in Tianjin, where Yan Fu was appointed as Provost after he returned from England. After graduation, Wu was sent to England and studied five years at the same school Yan Fu studied. When Wu became a translator, the two persons often exchanged ideas about translation by mail. Though researchers haven't found any hard evidence that could prove Wu's claim, we need to take this story seriously.

eighteenth-century trend of "loose" translation, Tytler proposed an idea of translation similar to Eugene Nida's dynamic equivalence. Tytler deems a good translation to be that "in which the merit of the original work is so completely transfused into another language, as to be distinctly apprehended, and as strongly felt, by a native of the country to which that language belongs, as it is by those who speak the language of the original" (*Tytler* 15-16). More importantly, he gives three "general laws" of a good translation that could instantiate his translation idea:

1. That the translation should give a complete transcript of the idea of the original work.

2. That the style and manner of writing should be of the same character with that of the original.

3. That the translation should have all the ease of the original composition. (16)

It is clear Yan Fu's three-word criteria for excellence in translation bear some resemblance to Tytler's three principles. Both Yan Fu and Tytler tried to master not only the "idea" but also the "style and manner" of the source text. Tytler's three principles roughly correspond to Yan Fu's *xin* (accuracy), *da* (comprehensibility), and *ya* (elegance). However, because of the shortage of historical evidence, whether or not Yan Fu was influenced directly by Tytler remains unclear. Yan Fu was highly unlikely to know Tytler's book from a Chinese source, because the book was first introduced to China in 1921 by Zheng Zhengduo. However, *Essays on the Principles of Translation* was a well-circulated treatise on translation and attained "celebrity in England" and had "some European popularity" (*Tytler* XXXI). During his stay in England from 1877 to 1879 as a navy science student, Yan Fu demonstrated a great interest in Western social science, literature and political systems. Guo Songtao (1818-1891), the Chinese ambassador to London at the time, was so impressed by Yan Fu's knowledge about Western learning that he recommended Yan Fu to the Qing court several times. It is well possible that Yan Fu had some contact with Tytler's ideas or books. The reason that Yan Fu did not mention this source could be that Yan Fu did not want to disturb his contemporary elite literati.

Yan Fu's *xin-da-ya* principles have had an enormous impact on subsequent Chinese translators. It is not an exaggeration to say that every Chinese translator after Yan Fu responds to his translation theorizing in one way or another. In his study on Yan Fu's three principles, Shen Surui documents as many as one hundred and nine interpretations on *xin*, *da*, and *ya* after the publishing of *Tian yan lun (Evolution and Ethics)* in 1898. Zou Zhenghuan put it in a simple way: "As a systematic theory on translation, 'Translation has to do three difficult things: accuracy, intelligibility, and elegance' has been accepted widely, despite the fact that there are different interpretations of what constitutes each of those terms" (527). I will go over some of the representative views on Yan Fu's principles.

Before the publishing of Yan Fu's book, Liang Qichao had read the draft translation, which motivated him to write immediately an article on translation to promote Yan Fu's book and translation method. Liang distinguished two strategies in translating Western books: one attempting at the beauty of Chinese at the expense of the meaning of Western texts, another one trying to bend the Chinese language towards the accurate expression of the source text. Liang prefers the second one and approves translation methods such as adding, deleting, and restructuring "for the sake of accuracy" (*Liang* 64). The second strategy is exemplified in Yan Fu's translation. Though Liang thought Yan Fu's three principles captured the nature of translation, he doubted that the three principles could be realized perfectly in a translation. Therefore, he thought Yan Fu listed the three principles in the order of priority from low to high.

A radical promoter of baihuawen (vernacular Chinese), Hu Shi nonetheless defends Yan Fu's use of classical Chinese: "At his time, it was not convenient to use vernacular Chinese, because if vernacular Chinese were used, no one would read translations. Eight-legged essay* style didn't fit translation either. So the style Yan Fu chose to use was a contingent choice" (*Hu* 115). Interestingly, though Hu Shi was certain that a classical Chinese transla*tion could achieve the excellences of xin, da,* and *ya,* he considered Yan Fu's translation in a "dead language" as comprehensible while translations of some fiction by Lu Xun and Zhou Zuoren could be counted as the model of Yan Fu's three principles.

Many scholars reached the same conclusion as Hu Shu and viewed Yan Fu's classic Chinese as a "dead language." The question of why he chose a "dead language" and why he proposed a principle for good translation remained unanswered. In fact, Yan Fu's *Tian yan lun (Evolution and Ethics)* was conditioned by the historical situation and literary conventions. In the next section, I discuss the political and literary influences on *Tian yan lun* by looking at the process of translating and publishing the book.

Publishing Tian yan lun

In 1813, Friedrich Schleiermacher published his influential treatise *On the Different Methods of Translating,* in which he distinguished two different ways of translation: "Either the translator leaves the writer alone as much as possible

---

* Eight-legged essay is a writing form with extreme restrictions on format, wording, and topic. In the Ming and Qing dynasties, candidates at civil examinations were required to write an eight-legged essay to explicate the Confucian classics.

and moves the reader toward the writer, or he leaves the reader alone as much as possible and moves the writer toward the reader" (*Schulte* 41-2). As a translator of theology, Schleiermacher prefers the first method in that an alienating method of translation could preserve real ideas and intentions of the sacred source texts. Dealing with a different kind of source text, Lin Shu adopted the other translation strategy with the hope of moving the writer to his elite Chinese readers.

It is now a truism to say that Yan Fu's choice was made out of his political and historical context. Scholars have long argued that the disastrous 1895 defeat of China to Japan galvanized Yan Fu's hibernated political enthusiasm. Right after the Chinese Beiyang Fleet suffered heavy losses against the Japanese, Yan Fu published a series of political essays in newspapers. One factor that led to Yan Fu's political enthusiasm is oftern neglected by his researchers. In addition to the humiliation felt by common Chinese, Yan Fu suffered more because many Chinese military officers were his classmates and friends back in the Fuzhou Naval Academy and the Greenwich Naval College. After the breakout of war, Yan Fu closely followed each battle. After the outright failure of the Chinese army, Yan Fu attacked the military and political systems and proposed a systematic reform. The translation of *Evolution and Ethics* stands as his first effort to fulfill his political proposals, namely that, "to strengthen the people's body", "to enlighten the people's mind," and "to renew the people's morality" (*Yan* 28). In addition to this macro-political model, Andre Lefevere provides us with a theory which makes subtle and close analysis possible. Viewing translation as a form of rewriting, Lefevere focuses on factors that systematically govern the selection, production, and reception of literary texts. Lefevere identifies three main factors: professionals within the literary system, patronage outside the literary system, and the dominant poetics. (1-10). Critics, reviewers, and teachers are professionals who affect the reception of a translation by examining its aesthetic and ideological qualities. Patronage demonstrates itself as "the powers (persons, institutions) that can further or hinder the reading, writing, and rewriting of literature" (*Lefevere* 15). Dominant poetics provide the translator with a literary repertoire which includes genres, symbols, leitmotif and prototypical situations and characters. According to Lefevere, translation is always carried out in the interaction between poetics and ideology. I next examine what poetic and political considerations were at work in Yan Fu's translation of *Evolution and Ethics* by tracing the process of its publishing.

As a profession, translation became increasingly connected with the daily life of the Chinese people after the forced opening of port-cities in 1840. However, the reputation of interpreters and translators remained very low. An open-minded scholar who advocated that China adopt Western technology, Feng Guifen (1809-1874), however, gave us an extremely negative account of Chinese interpreters in his article "On the Adoption of Western Learning." In his opinion, those interpreters were stupid, illiterate, and immoral, because they came from lower class families. Their translations were not able to capture the "mildness or severity of the original statement, its sense of urgency or lack of insistence." Unfortunately, Chinese officials had to rely on their inaccurate and preposterous interpretation when communicating with foreigners, because Chinese officials "from the governors down are completely ignorant of foreign countries" (*de Bary* 238).

Similarly, translators were despised by Chinese literati at that time. Ma Jianzhong (1845-1900), the author of the first Chinese grammar book, earned his degree at the École Libre des Sciences Politiques and had wonderful knowledge of French, English, Greek, and Latin.

Notwithstanding his background, he never translated a book in his life. In his petition to the Qing court for establishing a translation school, he describes the situation of the translators:

> Translators of today, with their rudimentary command of the foreign language, are unable to give the proper equivalents to render the nuances of meaning or archaisms of that language; or, though being well-schooled in a foreign language, are only capable of producing a version in Chinese that sounds provincial and slangy, which indicates that they have not yet been properly initiated into the art of translation…It can be seen, therefore, that those who are versed in a foreign language cannot express themselves in proper Chinese, while those who are masters of Chinese cannot understand the foreign language—little wonder the books thus translated are often found to be full of turns of phrase of mixed levels, styles and usages, expressions that are verbose, circumlocutory and erroneous.

> 今之譯者，大抵於外國之語言，或稍涉其藩籬，而其文字之微辭奧旨，與夫各國之古詞者，率茫然而未識其名稱；或僅通外國文字語言，而漢文則粗陋鄙俚，未窺門徑...蓋通洋文者不達漢文，通漢文者不達洋文，亦何怪夫所譯之書皆駁雜迂訛，為天下識者所鄙夷而訕笑也。

Yan Fu began his translation career in this historical context. According to Yan Fu's preface to *Tian yan lun (Evolution and Ethics)*, he started translating the book in the summer of 1896 and finished as late as October. Thomas Henry Huxley's *Evolution and Ethics* was based on a speech he had given at the University of Oxford in 1893 as the second of the annual Romanes lectures. When he published this lecture the same year he wrote a preface titled "Prolegomena" to refute his critics. The book was soon reprinted in 1894. Yan Fu never mentioned how he got hold of Huxley's newly published book, but he was not a stranger to evolutionist ideas. According to Guo Songtao, because evolutionism was a popular theory in England, Yan Fu read some Darwin, Spencer and Huxley at Greenwich Naval College (*Luo* 53). In his "Translator's Preface" to *qun xue shi yan*, his Chinese translation of Herbert Spencer's *Study of Sociology*, Yan Fu clearly stated that he had read this book in 1881, one year after he came back from England. Yan Fu's first draft of *Tian yan lun (Evolution and Ethics)* includes his preface, remarks on translation, and two chapters of translations: the first chapter is the translation of Huxley's *Prolegomena* and the second the translation of Huxley's lecture. Yan Fu made some changes to the original: *Prolegomena* contains 15 sections, while in Yan's translation there are 18 sections; Huxley's lecture is divided into 7 sections, while Yan made it into 17 sections. Though Yan Fu modified his translation several times before it was published, the basic structure of his translation remained unchanged. Another feature of Yan's translation is that he put his own notes and comments in the translation, a writing style that was used by the great Chinese historian Sima Qian (145-90 BCE) when he wrote *Shi ji* (Historical records). I discuss the history and implication of this style in the next section. Suffice it to say here that Yan Fu's translation strategy was influenced by traditional poetic conventions.

After Yan Fu finished his translation, he sent the draft to some friends for review. Upon receiving responses from the reviewers, Yan Fu made huge revisions on his first draft in 1897. He rewrote his preface, added many more notes and comments, restructured some sections, and deleted most Chinese idioms. From December 1897 to February 1898, parts of the new version of *Tian yan lun* were serialized on the *Guo wen hui bian* (Collections of National News), a supplement to the *Guo wen bao* (National News) focusing on translating Western news pieces. In early 1898, Lu Bi (1876-1967) printed Yan Fu's translation and sent Yan Fu a copy for more revision. The biggest change in this final revision was the addition of a title for each section. Wu Rulun suggested Yan Fu make this change and drafted all the titles for him. Wu also wrote a preface to the book that highly praised Yan Fu's contribution. In the summer of 1898, the final version of *Tian yan lun* was published by Lu Bi and became a popular book immediately.

Because Yan Fu sent his draft translation to some of his friends for review, his translation was circulated among some elite literati before its publication. Among those literati, Liang Qichao and Wu Rulun made significant contributions to Yan Fu's translation. Considering that Liang and Wu had different political stances, an interesting fact Yan Fu's researchers often neglect, Yan Fu's choice of reviewers was of historical and symbolic implications. Both Liang and Wu were open-minded Chinese literati, as opposed to conservatives in the late Qing political spectrum, in that they recognized the fact that the West was superior to China in certain ways and advocated learning from the West in order to strengthen China. But different understandings of what China needed to learn from the West divided the two into two different political camps, namely, the Yangwu camp and the reformist camp. After China was defeated by the British in the Opium War, some Qing officials concluded that the failure reflected the backwardness of military power in China, so that China needed to learn Western science and technology. Aiming at modernizing Chinese economy, especially its military power, these officials launched the Yangwu Movement or the Self-strengthening Movement and opened arsenals, factories, and shipyards in some big cities according to Western models. Ideologically, with a strong sense of cultural superiority, participating officials and literati generally observed the doctrine "Chinese learning for the substance, Western learning for the function," which was proposed by the Governor of Hubei and Hunan Zhang Zhidong (1837-1909), one of the main players in the Self-strengthening Movement. Wu Rulun was attached to this group of officials who wielded great political and ideological power. However, the defeat of China by Japan awakened some Chinese from the dream that technological modernization could strengthen China. As the prominent representatives, Kang Youwei and Liang Qichao called for a systematic reform that involved economical, political, legal, social, educational, and cultural systems. Those reformers believed that the West was superior to China in every regard and comprehensive reforms had to be carried out to imitate Western systems. Backed by Emperor Guangxu (1871-1908), the reformers undertook a short-lived Hundred Days' Reform Movement in 1898 that ended in a bloody *coup d'état* by conservatives. Despite the political failure, reformist ideas gained huge support from many Chinese literati. When Yan Fu solicited reviews from Wu Rulun and Liang Qichao, he was actually seeking support from the Yangwu camp and the reformist camp, one having great political power and another having moral and intellectual authority.

When Yan Fu sent Liang Qichao his translation and several political essays, he had not met Liang face to face. The only connection between them was a letter Liang had written Yan early that year discussing political reform. The reason Yan Fu sent his translation to Liang could be in response to Liang's letter. In addition, Yan Fu also wanted to seek a publication opportunity, though he only mentioned to Liang to publish his political essays. Yan Fu's early political essays in the *Shi bao* (Current News) drew a lot of attention from open-minded literati, but Yan Fu was regarded by many, such as premier Li Hongzhang, as only an expert in Western learning and thus was excluded from elite political circles. On the contrary, Liang Qichao had earned for himself national fame by petitioning the Qing emperor to start political reform in May 1895. Liang and his master Kang Youwei became the most outspoken voices for systematic reforms. At the time when Yan Fu sent his translation, Liang was serving as editor-in-chief of the *Shi wu bao* (Current Affairs), a newly founded newspaper that advocated reform ideas. Liang Qichao was obviously impressed by the ideas of evolution in Yan Fu's translation and gave the translation a high evaluation. Liang Qichao started immediately to propagate Darwinist ideas that he had learned from Yan's book and published several of Yan's political essays in his newpaper, but *Tian yan lun* (Evolution and Ethics) did not get the chance to appear on the *Shi wu bao*, because Liang was forced into exile to Japan after powerful conservatives thwarted the Hundred Days' Reform in 1898.

Unlike Liang Qichao, Wu Rulun (1840-1903) played a far more important role in Yan Fu's translation. Wu was known for his excellence in writing classic essays and regarded as the last master of the Tongcheng School. Because of the influence of Zeng Guofan (1811-1872) and Li Hongzhang (1823-1901), two most influential politicians in the late Qing era, Wu advocated educational reform and had a tolerant attitude towards Western culture. Yan Fu was a great admirer of Wu because Yan failed the Imperial examinations several times and was desperate to be recognized as a good classical essayist. That is why Yan Fu discussed his translation project with Wu and sent his translation to Wu for review. Wu did not disappoint Yan Fu. After he read Yan Fu's translation, he wrote to Yan, "Since China started to translate Western books, there is nothing comparable with [*Tian yan lun*]; no other translator could write this kind of wonderful essay. I admire you very much!" (Yan 1560). Besides this kind of lavish praise, Wu also gave detailed suggestions that prompted Yan Fu to revise his draft. Attempting to bring the original closer to its Chinese readers, Yan Fu tended to replace Western historical facts with Chinese ones. For example, when Huxley tried to explain the idea of justice, he used examples from *The Book of Job*, the Buddhist Sutras, the Psalmists and the Preacher of Israel, and the Tragic Poets of Greece. Then he writes, "What is a more common motive of the ancient tragedy in fact, than the unfathomable injustice of the nature of things" (59). In his first draft Yan Fu paraphrased this sentence as "People who have died in natural disasters outnumber those who have been killed by emperors Jie and Zhou."* Following this, Yan Fu elaborated this point by an expansive supplement to the translation:

> Is it true that every sin will be punished for what it deserves? What punishment did Chu Shangchen of the Spring and Autumn Period receive for his crime? He became the king; his descendants were knighted and enjoyed prosperity and happiness forever. Pan Chong was his accomplice in this crime by teaching Shangchen to kill his own father. But his descendants were respected and wealthy persons. Geng and Hui were poor and died very young. What crime did they commit? Huo and Zhi were rich and long lived. What achievement did they accomplish?**

---

* Jie is the last emperor of the Xia dynasty (2100-1600 BCE) and Zhou is the last emperor of the Shang dynasty (1600-1100 BCE). According to historical records and legends, the two emperors were extremely cruel to their people,which led to the overthrow of their regimes. Therefore, Jie and Zhou have become synonymous with cruelty and injustice in Chinese history.

** Shangchen was a prince of the kingdom Chu in the Spring and Autumn Period (770-476 BCE) and Pan Chong his private instructor. In order to become heir-apparent, Shangchen tricked his father into killing his premier who opposed the idea. After being placed the first in the line to the crown, Shangchen usurped the crown by forcing his father to commit suicide. Pan Chong was the mastermind behind Shangchen's crimes.

是豈皆惡而罰之所應加者哉？春秋之楚商
臣，其惡為何如惡耶？乃及其身為王者，子伯
諸侯，永世克祿；潘崇助之為虐，教人殺父弒
君，其胸中曾不芥蒂。然而其子孫纍業尊顯。
回耕何罪而貧夭？貨跖何功而富壽？ (1448)

Yan Fu's "translation" is a wonderful interpretation of
the original passage in a form similar to *lun*, a Chinese
literary style for argumentation. In his first draft, Yan Fu
more often than not cited passages from *Analects*, *Mencius*,
and the *Book of Change* in the above fashion. Wu Rulun
was firmly against this method and believed that translation needed to make bare the difference between Chinese
and Western cultures. In a letter to Yan Fu, Wu argued
that the ancient books and historical incidents in Huxley's
book "should be kept as Western names instead of being replaced with Chinese ones," because Huxley knew
nothing about Chinese history (*Wu* 144). At first glance,
Wu seemed to prefer a kind of foreignizing translation
strategy, as Venuti promoted. In fact, the ideal translation
model in Wu's mind was that of the Five Dynasties (907-
960), whose prominent representative was Kumarajiva.
As I mentioned before, the Five Dynasties translators of
Buddhist Scriptures abandoned the popular literary translation method adopted by translators of previous dynasties.
The general requirement for a good translation was shifted
from emphasis on accuracy to highlighting aesthetic quality. Kumarajiva's translations were highly valued because
he was good at turning the lengthy and dull original into
concise and stylistic Chinese. Besides the aesthetic prefer-
ence, another quality caught Wu's attention when he tried
to persuade Yan Fu to keep the original names and historical incidents. Wu noticed that one could easily distinguish
a translation in the Five Dynasties from a creation, because translations differed greatly from original works by
Chinese literati in both style and form. Moreover, because

of the reworking of the original, a translation would not be a copy of the original and inevitably became a particular form. In other words, stylistically speaking, a translation should be a hybrid that is foreign to both the original and the target language. These are the two sides of the same coin. As a result, Wu told Yan, "Because European languages are completely different from ours, in order to translate them you'd better create a special style" (*Wu* 235). In order to preserve foreign qualities, Wu did not want Yan Fu to insert Chinese sages and classics into the original. The political implication for this method was that it could break the myth that Western history and wisdom can be seamlessly transferred into Chinese history and wisdom, a myth believed by many conservatives who refused to learn from the West. Because of Wu Rulun's forceful argument, in his final version Yan Fu deleted almost all the replacements of Chinese historical incidents with the foreign ones and followed closely the original on this matter.

In responding to Yan Fu's question about the style of translation, Wu explicated his idea on translation as a stylistic hybrid. Yan Fu made a comparison between European histories and Chinese chronological records, then asked Wu's opinion about using narrative styles in Chinese historical records to translate European history books. Wu Rulun felt that Western biographies were too trivial and translations of them needed to adopt the concise narrative style exemplified by Sima Qian. If a translation made no deletions and reconstructions to the original for the sake of concision, its acceptability would be compromised. While Wu endorsed Sima Qian's historical narrative style, he deemed fictional narrative to be an inappropriate model in the translation of European history books. Chinese writers produced many fictional biographies of legendary and historical figures. Because of their fictive nature, their narrative style could not be used as the model for translations of history. However, not every Chinese historical narrative, argued Wu, was compatible with this kind of translation. A "particular style" (*Wu* 235) should be created out of the tradition of Chinese history to achieve the goal of a comprehensive translation of a Western history book. It was well known that Sima Qian created the narrative style that historian's comments were affixed to historical records. If one considers Wu Rulun's promotion of Sima Qian's narrative style, the way that Yan Fu made his comments and notes in his translation would come as no surprise. Wu's call for a "special style" encouraged Yan Fu to explore his own ways to do translation.

In the first section, I discussed the importance and complexity of one of Yan Fu's three principles, *ya*. As the last master of the classic essayist of the Tongcheng School, Wu Rulun pressed an unmistakable mark on Yan Fu's understanding of *ya*. Yan Fu was once faced with a dilemma in translating Huxley, as he formulated in a letter to Wu: "My translation is in pursuit of elegance, but there are always some improper words. Changing them, you lose accuracy; following them, you lose language purity. This is a really difficult choice" (*Yan* 1419). Without any hesitation, Wu voted for the preservation of elegance: "My humble opinion is: Instead of hurting the language purity, accuracy could be compromised" (635). The Tongcheng School stressed the elucidation of the article's purpose and the beauty of the wording. Because conciseness and naturalness were valued, essayists of the Tongcheng School preferred an archaic style and refused to use any fancy and vulgar words. According to Wu, an essay should be written in the language used by Chinese official-literati who maintained the language purity. Wu conceded that classic works, such as *Shi ji (Records of the Grand Historian)* and *Zhuangzi*, used slang and vulgar words, but those kinds of words could be viewed as elegant since they were used by all writers at their time. Wu seemed to suggest that *ya* (elegance) was a historical concept, and a group of literati maintained what constituted *ya* at a historical period. Yan Fu's idea on *ya* differs from Wu's on this issue. Yan Fu agreed with Wu that *ya* as a style was solely decided by literati; this partly explains why Yan Fu claimed that using classic words and style could promote the acceptance of his translation. Unlike Wu, Yan Fu instantiated the essence of *ya* in pre-Qin writings and words. However, the difference between the two was not as big as it seemed to be. Though writers under the rubric of the Tongcheng School shared some basic principles, such as precision and naturalness, they disagreed with each other on who was the ideal writer. In short, Wu shaped Yan Fu's understanding of *ya* and paved the way for Yan Fu to choose his translation strategy.

Not only did Wu Rulun prepare Yan Fu intellectually, but he also took part in Yan Fu's translation. In Yan Fu's draft, there was no title for each section. Wu feared this violated the convention of classic essays; therefore, he composed all 35 titles for Yan. When Yan Fu finally published his translation, he adopted 28 of the titles Wu had made for him. Yan Fu once recalled Wu's role in his translations, "Whenever I finished my translation I sent the draft to Mr. Wu of Tongcheng. Though he was old, he could catch immediately the gist of the translation. My writing benefited from his revisions. Therefore, after I finished a translation, I always asked him to read it and write a preface" (*Yan* 126-127). Wu also made an effort to sponsor the publication of *Tian yan lun*. Because of the shortage of funding, the *Guo wen hui bian* (Collections of National News), in which *Tian yan lun* was serialized, ceased to function after only seven issues. At the request of Yan Fu, Wu wrote to one of his friends who worked for the governor of Tianjin in the hope of receiving publication funding. At that time, newspaper and publishing industries were mainly dominated by private and foreign capital. The government did not sponsor any publication that was not associated with governmental institutions. Wu's effort ultimately failed.

In a sense, Wu Rulun offered an "undifferentiated" patronage for Yan Fu's translation of *Evolution and Ethics* because he assumed all three responsibilities of patronage, including, as Lefevere has pointed out, ideological, economic, and status components. As an advocate of the self-strengthening movement who once worked for two prominent politicians, Wu appreciated Yan Fu's new ideas and introduced his translation to various political figures. In the conflict between conservatives and reform-minded officials, Wu's recommendation promoted Yan Fu's reputation as a reformer and guaranteed the acceptance of his translation. Though Wu did not sponsor the publication of *Tian yan lun*, he did try to find government funding for Yan Fu. However, with the defeat of China in a variety of wars with foreigners, the power of the Qing government was restricted to the extent that it was not able to act as an omnipotent sponsor. Wu's failure indicated the coming of the era of the "differentiated" patronage. Wu's lavish praise of Yan Fu and his translation greatly improved Yan Fu's status in the literary circle. Yan Fu never received any degree from the Imperial Examinations. He was so frustrated that he regretted he had studied only Western learning. In his preface to *Tian yan lun*, Wu Rulun not only showed his respect for Yan Fu's solid knowledge about the West, but also praised his translation as one that reads like a pre-Qin classic essay. After that, Yan Fu was recognized as a talented classic essayist and established his status in the late Qing literary scene. Wu Rulun was so indispensable in Yan Fu's translation activities that Yan Fu lamented "No one else in the world can write a preface to my book" after the death of Wu Rulun in 1904 (*Yan* 127).

The above discussion has shown that Yan Fu benefited greatly from Liang Qichao and Wu Rulun during the process of translating *Tian yan lun*. In fact, the benefit was mutual, because both Liang and Wu learned so much from Yan Fu's translation that they changed their political ideas and worldviews. Compared with many of his contemporaries, Wu Rulun was open-minded, even heretical, and showed great interest in the West. He promoted Western leaning and favored the policy that allowed Chinese students to study abroad. As a matter of fact, Wu came in contact with Western learning only after he worked for Zeng Guofan as a personal aide in 1866. The reason Zeng chose Wu was that Wu had demonstrated his concrete knowledge about classics and possessed a staunch Confucian ambition to save the world with Confucius's teachings. A participant in the Self-strengthening Movement, he was exposed to Western learning through government documents, newspapers, and translated books as well as personal experiences with foreigners. Though Wu witnessed the power of Western science and technologies and admitted the necessity of studying Western learning, he insisted that the Self-strengthening Movement focus on technology, and that Confucianism stand as the fundamental ideology. In a word, the conservative dogma "Learn the strong techniques of the barbarians in order to control the barbarians" governed Wu when he handled issues related to Western learning. The basic logic inherent in this dogma was that China was still the center of the world and Westerners were like some barbarians of the old days but with some advanced technologies. Wu shared with Zeng Guofan, Li Hongzhang, and Zhang Zhidong the idea that the challenge posed by Westerners was unprecedented in the long Chinese history; he never thought of the fate of China as a death-or-survival struggle in a world where China was not the centre. Yan Fu's *Tian yan lun (Evolution and Ethics)* irreversibly transformed Wu Rulun's views of the world and China. In his preface to *Tian yan lun*, Wu recounted the history in this way:

> Based on the two concepts of "natural selection" and "struggle for survival," the evolution theory traces the origin of natural things and documents the development of animals and plants…Huxley thinks that nature cannot work alone and it is important for men to control nature. In order to control nature, humans must reach the limit of their potentials and maintain their domination every day. In so doing, one's country can exist forever and his race won't become extinct.

> 其學以天擇、物競二義，綜萬匯之本原，考動植之蕃耗...赫胥黎氏起而盡變故說，以為天不可獨任，要貴以人持天。以人持天，必究極乎天賦之能，使人治日及乎新，而後其國永存，而種族賴以不墜，是之謂與天爭勝。 (*Yan* 1317)

The picture of the world Yan Fu drew in his translation opened Wu's eyes and shook his comfortable assumption that the Dao of Heaven and Confucian doctrines remain unchanged. For the first time Wu learned that history advances in the battle between nature and humans and like Westerners, Chinese are only one of the races that struggle for their survival.

Translation as rewriting

In his preface to *Tian yan lun (Evolution and Ethics)*, Yan Fu elaborated on how he did the translation. He told his unilingual readers that Chinese translation could not follow the original construction thoroughly because of the differences between the two languages: "Terms in Western language texts are defined as they occur, somewhat similar to digressions in Chinese. What comes after elaborates what goes before and completes the sense and structure. A sentence in a Western language consists of from two or three words to tens or hundreds of words" (1321). What he did was to first read and digest the whole original text, and then rewrite it in the best Chinese manner he could produce. In cases when it was difficult to convey both the profound content and involved style, Yan Fu correlated "what precedes and what follows to bring out the theme," because his efforts were made to achieve comprehensibility (1322). This explains why Yan Fu put his name on the title page of his translation not as translator, but as one who "paraphrased the gist [of the original]."

The great difficulty that challenged Yan Fu throughout his translation project was to find accurate Chinese words for terms that were completely foreign to Chinese culture. He went on to explain his dilemma: "New theories have been advanced in quick succession, giving rise to a profusion of new terms. No such terms could be found in Chinese. Though some Chinese expressions approximate the original, there are yet discrepancies. Confronted with such a situation, a translator can only use his own judgment and coin a term according to the sense. But this is easier said than done" (1322). One example could be used to shed light on the extra work he needed when choosing an existing Chinese expression among many candidates. He recalled how he had finally decided on the translation of the simple word "prolegomena" after he had discussed it with Xia Zengyou and Wu Rulun many times. According to Yan Fu, he first translated "prolegomena" into *zhi yan* (words in a wine-glass), an expression first used by the great Chinese philosopher Zhuangzi (370-301 BCE), meaning one's truthful utterances.* Chinese literati of later

---

* In Zhuangzi's terminology, *zhi yan* 卮言 exists in relation to *yu yan* 寓言 and chong yan 重言. These are three styles to express the author's ideas in one's writing. In *yu yan*, the author's intentions are revealed by legends, tales, and stories of nonhumans. In *chong ya*, the author expresses himself

generations generally use this term to refer to their own works. Xia Zengyou (1863-1924), an active scholar and a good friend of Yan's, suggested xuan tan (metaphysical talks) as a replacement since he deemed *zhi yan* a banal usage. Xia's suggestion *xuan tan* recalled a Buddhist term referring to the introductory passage before the scripture text. Wu Rulun, however, thought *xuan tan* was a Buddhist cliché and suggested Yan insert a title for each section instead of translating the word "prolegomena." Yan Fu didn't regard *xuan tan* as a proper translation because it functioned as a summary in Buddhist texts. Finally, Yan Fu decided to coin a new Chinese term *dao yan* (introductory words), which became a popular phrase still used today. Yan Fu spent a lot of time and energy looking for proper expressions in Chinese classics; in his preface he claimed, "The determination of a term often took a full month's pondering. I leave it to the discerning and wise to commend or condemn me" (*Hsu* 6). Judging by the afterlife of his multiple new terms, Yan Fu's choices have in general been condemned by history, as only a few are still in use.

To help the Anglophone reader understand Yan Fu's strategies in the translation of T. H. Huxley's *Evolution and Ethics*, I refer to his translation of the first section of "Prolegomena" as an example. By juxtaposing the original, Yan Fu's translation, and my back translation of Yan Fu into English, I attempt to give a clear picture of what Yan Fu has done to the original for readers who do not know Chinese. Since my back translation tries to reproduce Yan Fu semantically, it can be called literal translation.

---

by citing others' writings, sayings, and stories. *zhi yan* refers to a style that the author's argument is in accordance with natural principles. Every piece of Zhuangzi's works usually adopts all three styles.

The annotation system I use is as following:

~~English~~: Omission   <u>English</u>: Error

{ }: pre-Qin expressions [ ]: Paraphrase (): Addition

EVOLUTION ~~AND ETHICS~~

PROLEGOMENA

I.

~~It may be safely assumed that,~~ two thousand years ago, before Caesar set foot in southern Britain, the whole country-side visible from the windows of the room in which I write, was in what is called "the state of nature." ~~Except, it may be,~~ by raising a few sepulchral mounds, such as those which still, here and there, break the flowing contours of the downs, man's hands had made no mark upon it; ~~and the thin veil of~~ vegetation which overspread the broad-backed heights and the shelving sides of the coombs was unaffected by his industry. The native grasses and weeds, the scattered patches of gorse, contended with one another for the possession

天演论上

导言一

（察变）

赫胥黎独处一室之中，在英伦之南，背山而面野。槛外诸境，历历如在几下。乃｛悬想｝二千年前，当（罗马大将）恺彻未到时，此间有何景物。计惟有｛天造草昧｝，人功未施，其借征人境者，不过几处荒坟，散见坡陀起伏间。而灌木丛林，蒙茸山麓，未经删治如今者，则无疑也。

怒生之草，交加之藤，势如争长相雄，各据一抔壤土，

On Evolution Part One

Introduction
One (Observation
of Change)

Huxley stays alone in a room that is located in southern Britain and that is behind a mountain while facing the plain. Everything outside of the windows is vividly clear. Then [he] {speculates} that two thousand years ago before (the Roman general) Caesar had arrived, what was it like here? It was only like {the beginning of the nature} and men made no marks. The things upon which men touched were a few tombs that dotted the contours of the hills. It was undoubted that the bushes and forest that covered the hills hadn't been trimmed and cut till today. Lush grasses and scattered vines contended with one another to thrive. Every one of them possessed a bit of soil. They of the scanty surface soil; they fought against the droughts of summer, the frosts of winter, and the furious gales which swept, with unbroken force, <u>now from the Atlantic</u>, and now from the North Sea, at all times of the year; ~~they filled up, as they best might, the gaps made in their ranks by~~ all sorts of underground and overground animal ravagers. One year with another, an average population, the floating balance of the unceasing struggle for existence among the indigenous plants, maintained itself. ~~It is as little to be doubted,~~ that an essentially similar state of nature prevailed, ~~in this region, for many thousand years before the coming of Caesar; and there is no assignable reason for denying~~ [that it might continue to exist through an equally prolonged futurity, except for the intervention of man.

Reckoned by our customary standards of duration, the native vegetation, like the "everlasting hills" which it

夏与畏日争，冬与严霜争，四时之内，飘风怒吹，或西发西洋，或东起北海，旁午交扇，无时而息。

上有鸟兽之践啄，下有蚁蝝之啮伤，憔悴孤虚，旋生旋灭，干枯顷刻，莫可究详。是｛离离者｝亦各尽天能，以自存种族而已。数亩之内，战事炽然，强者后亡，弱者先绝。年年岁岁，偏有留遗，未知始自何年，更不知止于何代。苟人事不施其间，则｛莽莽榛榛｝，长此互相吞并，混逐蔓延面已，而诘之者谁耶。

fought against sun flare in summer and against frosts in winter. The wind, coming either westward from the Western Sea or eastward from the Northern Sea, blew vehemently in four seasons and all day long without stopping. Because birds and animals from overground pecked and picked and ants and bugs from underground wrecked and destroyed, [grasses and vines] withered quickly after they sprouted. It was impossible to study this process in detail. Therefore, {everything} tried to realize its potential in order to maintain its race and ethnicity. Within several square feet, battles were fought fervently; the strong survived and the weak died. There have been survivals since years. It could never know when this had started and how long it would continue to exist. If there were no intervention of man, those grasses and vines would fight against each other forever and spread all over. Who would blame [those battles]! The

92

clothes, seems a type of permanence.] The little Amarella Gentians, which abound in some places to-day, are the descendants of those that were trodden underfoot, by the prehistoric savages who have left their flint tools, about, here and there; and they followed ancestors which, in the climate of the glacial epoch, probably flourished better than they do now. [Compared with the long past of this humble plant, all the history of civilized men is but an episode.]

Yet nothing is more certain than that, ~~measured by the liberal scale of time-keeping of the universe,~~ this present state of nature, however it may seem to have gone and to go on for ever, is but a fleeting phase of her infinite variety; merely the last of the series of changes which the earth's surface has undergone in the course of the millions of years of its existence. Turn back a square foot of the thin turf, and the solid foundation of the land, exposed

英之南野，黄芩之种为多，此自未有记载以前，{草衣石斧之民}所采撷践踏者，（兹之所见），其苗裔耳。邃古之前，坤枢未转，

英伦诸岛乃属冰天血海之区，此物能寒，法当较今尤茂。[此区区一小草耳，若迹其祖始，远及洪荒，则三古以还年代方之，犹瀼渴之水，比诸大江，不啻小支而已。]

故事有决无可疑者，则天道变化，不主故常是已。特自皇古迄今，为变概渐，浅人不察，遂有天地不变之言。实则今兹所见，乃自不可穷诘之变动而来。{京垓年岁之中，每每员舆正不知}几移几换而成此最后之奇。且继今以往，陵谷变迁，又属可知之事，此地学不刊之说也。（假其惊怖斯言，则索证

gentians that abound in southern Britain were picked and trodden by {the people wearing savage clothes and using stone axes }before the recorded history. What [Huxley] sees today is the descendants of those gentians. Long long ago, the nature was in chaos. Britain isles were still an area with the icy sky and the bloody sea. Gentians were hardy and should have flourished better than today. [If we trace the origin of this tiny grass, it goes back to the chaos. If we measure [its age] by the frame of the history since the three Chinese sages, it is like comparing a drop of water with a river.] Therefore, one unquestionable principle is that the Dao of the Heaven changes constantly. However, since human history the changes have undergone so slow that ignorant people couldn't notice them. That's why they think the heaven and the earth remain unchanged. The truth is what we see today comes from incessant in cliffs of chalk five hundred feet high on the adjacent shore, yields full assurance of a time when the sea covered the site of the "everlasting hills"; and when the vegetation of what land lay nearest, was as different from the present Flora of the Sussex downs, as that of Central Africa now is. No less certain is it that, between the time during which [the chalk was formed and that at which the original turf came into existence, thousands of centuries elapsed, in the course of which, the state of nature of the ages during which the chalk was deposited, passed into that which now is, by changes so slow that, in the coming and going of the generations of men, had such witnessed them, the contemporary, conditions would have seemed to be unchanging and unchangeable.]

[But it is also certain that, before the deposition of the chalk, a vastly longer period had elapsed; throughout which it is easy

正不在远。）试向立足处所，掘地深逾寻丈，将逢垩灰，以是（垩灰），知其地之古必为海。盖垩灰为物，乃蠃蚌积叠而成，若用显镜察之，其掩旋尚多完具者，使是地不前为海，此〔恒河沙数蠃蚌者胡从来乎？沧海扬尘，非诞说矣。〕

且地学之家，历验各种疆石，知动植庶品，率皆递有变迁。特为变至微，其迁极渐，即假吾人

changes. {In the course of the millions of years, the earth} had changed many times before it reached the last phase of miracle. Moreover, geology has proved that we now can understand changes of the rivers and mountains. (If one is surprised by this theory, proofs could be found nearby.) Dig tens of meters deep the place where you stand, you will find chalk. Based on the chalk, you can conclude this place was a sea in the ancient time. This is because chalk is made of weak and dead turfs. If you put a piece of chalk under a microscope, you will see many intact turfs. If this place wasn't a sea before, where did the countless turfs come from? That sea changed into soil isn't an absurd theory. After they examined all kinds of fossils, Geologists learnt that all animals and vegetation had experienced evolution. But because the changes happened very slowly, even if we were as long-lived as Pengzu and Laozi, we couldn't to follow the traces of the same process of ceaseless modification and of the internecine struggle for existence of living things;]~~and that even when we can get no further back, it is not because there is any reason to think we have reached the beginning, but because the trail of the most ancient life remains hidden, or has become obliterated.~~

Thus that state of nature of the world ~~of plants which we began by considering, is far from possessing the attribute of permanence. Rather its very essence is impermanence. It may~~ have lasted twenty or thirty thousand years, it may last for twenty or thirty thousand years more, without obvious change; but, as surely as it has followed upon a very different state, so it will be followed by an equally different condition. [That which endures is not one or another association of living forms, but the process of which the cosmos is the product, and of which these are among the transitory

彭、聃之寿，而亦由暂观久，潜移弗知；是犹｛蟪蛄不识春秋，朝菌不知晦朔｝，遽以不变名之，真｛瞽说｝也。故知不变一言，决非天运，而悠久成物之理，转在变动不居之中。

是当前之所见，经廿年、卅年而革焉可也，更二万年、三万年而革亦可也，特据前事推将来，为变方长，未知所极而已。虽然天运变矣，而有不变者行乎其中。

不变惟何？是名"天演"。以天演为体，而其用有二：曰物竞，曰天择。此万物莫不然，而于有生之类为尤著。（物竞者，物争自存也，

notice them. This is like {cicadas don't understand the concept of spring and autumn, and fungi have no idea of month.} If they think nature is unchangeable, it is only {the theory of the blind.} So now we know that the idea of unchangeable nature isn't true. What we see today will change after either twenty some years later or twenty thousands some years later. We predict future on the basis of the knowledge about the past. The thing is it takes time for change to happen, so we don't know its limit. However changes the Dao of nature undergoes, there remains something unchanged. What's this unchangeable thing? It's called "evolution." There are two functions of evolution: one is struggle for existence, another one natural selection. This principle is applied invariably to everything in the world, especially living creatures. Struggle for existence is a creature battles against others. Whether or not it survives depends on expressions. And in the living world, one of the most characteristic features of this cosmic process is the struggle for existence, the competition of each with all, the result of which is the selection, that is to say, the survival of those forms which, on the whole, are best adapted, to the conditions which at any period obtain; and which are, therefore, in that respect, and only in that respect, the fittest. The acme reached by the cosmic process in the vegetation of the downs is seen in the turf, with its weeds and gorse. Under the conditions, they have come out of the struggle victorious; and, by surviving, have proved that they are the fittest to survive.]

以一物以与物物争，或存或亡，而其效则归于天择。天择者，物争焉而独存。则其存也，必有其所以存，必其所得于天之分，自致一己之能，与其所遭值之时与地，及凡周身以外之物力，有其相谋相剂者焉。）夫而后独免于亡，而足以自立也。而自其效观之，若是物特为天之所厚而择焉以存也者，夫是之谓天择。天择者择于自然，虽择而莫之择，犹物竞之无所争，而实天下之至争也。（斯宾塞尔曰："天择者，存其最宜者也。"）夫物既争存矣，而天又从其争之后而择之，一争一择，而变化之事出矣。

the working of natural selection. (Natural selection means only one creature survives the struggles among many creatures for existence. The one who survives has its reasons: it is bestowed gifts by nature and develops its specialties. The time and place where it stays and the forces around it are harmonious, therefore, are conductive to its existence.) Due to these reasons, this very creature doesn't die and can survive. In effect, natural selection is nature selects those born gifted to survive. Because nature selects from natural creatures, natural selection isn't a selection. It's like struggle for existence is the highest form of struggle only because nothing struggles against it. (Spencer says, "Natural selection is to preserve the fittest.") Creatures struggle for their existence, and nature selects from those struggles. Change come from this kind of struggle and selection.

In the discussion of Lin Shu's translation of Harriet Beecher Stowe's *Uncle Tom's Cabin*, I showed that Lin Shu constantly practiced deletion from the original when it came to the parts that were irrelevant to the development of plot. Similarly, deletions are immediately visible from the above sample translation. One can conclude that deleting is also a translation technique practiced by Yan Fu. He obviously deleted some foreign geographic names, such as "Central Africa", "the Atlantic" and "Sussex". A close reading tells us the fact that Yan Fu tends to delete conjunctions and accessory words, such as "It may be safely assumed that", "it may be", "however it may seem to", and so on and so forth. These expressions are common in connecting sentences or paragraphs and betray a sense of precision in a scientific text. Yan Fu deleted these words partly because he tried to achieve the ideal style of brevity while staying loyal to the original semantically. Another reason for Yan Fu to do this was his effort to transform the original into Chinese grammatically and stylistically. Grammatically, compared with the English language, the passive tense appears less frequently in Chinese. As a consequence, expressions like "It may be safely assumed that" are hard to translate into classical Chinese. By omitting those expressions, Yan Fu avoided confronting Chinese grammar and saved himself some trouble. Stylistically, one of the conspicuous features of classic essays is the habitual use of parallelism, namely, that sentences are balanced in terms of the number of characters and word order. It is difficult to form a couplet if those conjunctions and accessory words are translated. Yan Fu's translation of the second sentence reads like a sentence from a Chinese classic because he omits expressions "except", "it may be", and "such as those which still" and arranges his translation with couplet-like sentences.

I mentioned before that Yan Fu was inclined to rearrange the structure of the original for the sake of comprehensibility. The rearrangement of the original was more often than not combined with his strategy of deletion. Since the original text is Huxley's speech on a scientific subject, the first-person singular subject pronoun "I" is implicitly or explicitly visible from the very beginning. In the translation, the first-person subject in the original was rearranged as the third-person subject that fits in the narrative stereotype of Chinese historical records. For his well-educated readers, the book reads like a biography because Yan Fu started his narration in the translation with "Huxley" and turned a scientific speech into an account of a person named Huxley. This impression was definitely reinforced by Yan Fu's rearrangement of the structure: instead of following the original structure that is full of clauses, Yan Fu's translation of the first paragraph consists of short, couplet-like sentences that do not correspond to the original one by one. However, his translation can still be categorized as an "acceptable translation" in the sense it is oriented primarily towards the norms of the target culture (*Toury* 56-57). Also, his translation is acceptable because the basic meaning of the original is preserved. A comparison of the original to my back translation attests to Yan Fu's semantic accuracy. In sum, deletion was generally used by Yan Fu to sinicize his translation grammatically and stylistically. If Lin Shu's constant and massive use of deletion was due mainly to his lack of foreign language capacity, Yan Fu practiced the strategy of deletion moderately to serve his stylistic ends. More importantly, the achievement of style was not at the price of accuracy.

Addition was another strategy Yan Fu used in his translation. There were several reasons for him to add something in his translation. One reason was to introduce basic information to his Chinese readers who were unfamiliar with Western history. Caesar was well known to Huxley's audience, but he was virtually unknown to Yan Fu's readers. What Yan Fu did was to add "the Roman general" before Caesar in the translation. Addition was also a good choice when Yan Fu wanted to elaborate on the points Huxley had made in the text. One proper example can be found in the translation of "unceasing struggle for existence." Yan Fu's translation of this phrase is "battles were fought fervently; the strong survived and the weak died. There have been survivals for years." The Chinese translation, consisting of two couplets full of poetic beauty, emphasizes the cruelty of the struggle and the difficulty of survival. His readers could easily find its resemblance to other historical accounts of battles. The deep sense of history emanating from this additional elaboration not only furnished the translation with literary qualities inherent in traditional genres, but also reinforced the "unceasing" nature of the "struggle for existence" suggested by Huxley. Yan Fu also used the strategy of additions when he made a summary of the original argument. Throughout the whole speech, Huxley never used the term "natural selection," a key concept in evolutionism. Instead, he used the term "selection," which referred to the survival of the fittest that was "best adapted, to the conditions." Yan Fu distilled what Huxley really meant and translated "selection" as *tian ze*, literally meaning "heavenly selection." Moreover, to clarify and foreground Huxley's central argument on evolution, Yan Fu added a summary in, once again, couplet-like sentences: "There are two functions of evolution: one is struggle for existence, another one natural selection."

The application of cultural decorations was Yan Fu's strategy to deal with cultural differences between China and the West. By cultural decoration I mean Yan Fu's use of expressions full of cultural connotations when translating fairly neutral statements. Take the original sentence

"Compared with the long past of this humble plant, all the history of civilized men is but an episode." Yan Fu's translation goes like this: "If we measure [its age] by the frame of the history since the three Chinese sages, it is like comparing a drop of water with a river." Firstly, Yan Fu has inserted a time concept that was only meaningful in the Chinese culture. According to Confucian tradition, the period of the three Chinese sages refers to the long process of the formation of *The Book of Change*, the oldest Chinese philosophical book. It gradually became the designation of ancient times. Secondly, the original comparison between the histories of "humble plant" and "civilized men" was transformed into the one between "water" and "river." The reason behind this change was obvious to all educated Chinese, not just Chinese literati who were well versed in classics. Because when ancient Chinese philosophers discussed the relationship between emptiness and fullness or long and short, they preferred the comparison between "water" and "river" or between "river" and "ocean."* Thirdly, what Yan Fu did here was a kind of overtranslation because the original sentence was only a scientific statement of universal characteristics. Rather than replicating the original tone, Yan Fu decorated his translation with unsophisticated poetical beauty and rich philosophical association. The same strategy was at work when Yan Fu cited in his translation legendary figures, such as Pengzu and Laozi, and sentences about cicadas and fungi from Zhuangzi's work.

---

* The comparison can be found in the works of famous philosophers such as Zhuangzi, Mozi (470-390 BCE), and Xunzi (310-237 BCE). One example is Xunzi's "Exhortation to Learning," a classic text that is still in the middle school textbook. In the text, Xunzi argues that knowledge comes from accumulation of bits of information. One of his supporting evidence is that "Rivers and seas cannot be formed without the accumulation of drops of water and creeks."

All the translation strategies I have discussed demonstrate that Yan Fu aimed at aestheticing his translation according to the norms of traditional poetics. A devotee to reform ideas, Yan Fu never hid his political ambition in translating *Evolution and Ethics*. Therefore, a politicizing strategy did play an indispensable role in his translation. In translating "One year with another, an average population, the floating balance of the unceasing struggle for existence among the indigenous plants, maintained itself", Yan Fu uses "race and ethnicity" to translation "itself", that is, every one of the "indigenous plants." This was probably only a mistranslation and we shouldn't read too much into it. However, there are reasons for us to believe that Yan Fu's choice was based on political considerations. As I discussed before, following the cited sentence, Yan Fu added two couplet-like sentences to emphasize the cruelty of battle. He also chose a Chinese term meaning "war" or "battle" to translate "struggle" at this particular place, while a neutral Chinese term equivalent to "struggle" is used to translate "struggle" in all other places. Similarly, Yan Fu always chose the Chinese word meaning "object" to translate "men", "animals", "vegetations", and "plants." Yan Fu's calculated use of "race and ethnicity" was an understandable reading of evolutionism for someone whose nation was in a life-and-death situation, but it also marked the difference between Yan Fu and Huxley. Though the "survival of the fittest" doctrine is susceptible to the malicious interpretation that evolution leads to questionable ethics, Huxley separates man's morality sharply from Nature and maintains that morality governs the function of human society. That's why he named his book *Evolution and Ethics*. However, Yan Fu's reading of evolutionism leaned towards social Darwinism in that he applied the Darwinian biological ideas of "natural selection" to the social realm. The "struggle for existence" among plants and animals was conveniently interpreted as wars in human society, and the "survival of the fittest" was seamlessly integrated into a nationalistic discourse on the dangers for Chinese as a race. In Yan Fu's political agenda, survival is on the top while ethics has no place. That's why he translated Huxley's *Evolution and Ethics* into *Tian yan lun*, literally meaning "On Evolution."

Yan Fu's politicizing strategy and aestheticing strategy are interdependent and work hand in hand to produce a translation meeting the principles of *xin (accuracy)*, *da (comprehensibility)*, and *ya (elegance)*. Whether Yan Fu added, deleted, or decorated in his translation was a matter of an aesthetic problem. Classical poetics served as Yan Fu's highest aesthetic standard. His embrace of classics won him political and poetical sponsorship that assured his literary fame, which in turn facilitated the wide spread of his political ideas. By politicizing key concepts in his translation, Yan Fu allowed foreign ideas to sneak into Chinese culture and literature without destroying the traditional cultural system. Through Yan Fu's classical style translation, evolutionism, especially the strain of social Darwinism, took root in traditional Chinese literati. Since then, the question of the Chinese as a race has surfaced and made its way to the political agendas of reformists, conservatives, and revolutionists. Both Lin Shu's translation of *Uncle Tom's Cabin* and Yan Fu's translation of *Evolution and Ethics* shared the same concern for the identity of the Chinese people. Though the genres of their originals were different, the two translators made the same decision on using classic Chinese to translate new ideas. On the contrary, Liang Qichao tried to change the hierarchy of the traditional literary system and experimented with a new language in writing and translating. I discuss Liang Qichao's literary and political ideas in the next chapter.

Chapter Three

ALLEGORICAL NEW CHINA: LIANG QICHAO'S THEORY OF POLITICAL FICTION AND TRANSLATIONS

In his study of Qing intellectual trends, Liang Qichao recounts how he overcomes the traditional influence on his writing style by coming to terms with a new style full of "colloquialisms, verses, and foreign expressions":

> Liang Qichao had never liked the ancient-style writing of the Tongcheng school. When he started to learn writing when he was young, he had followed the style of the late Han, Wei, and Qin, and it particularly attended to dignity and refinement, but now he liberated himself from it, and tried to be plain and fluently expressive. He interlarded his writings with colloquialisms, verses, and foreign expressions fairly frequently, letting his pen flow freely and without restraint. Scholars hastened to imitate his style and it became known as the New-Style Writing; however, the older generation was resentful of it and slandered it as heretical. Nevertheless, his style had a clear structure and the flow of his pen was often full of feeling, with a special charm over the reader.

啟超夙不喜桐城派古文。幼年為文，學晚
漢魏晉，頗尚矜鍊。至是自解放，務為平易暢
達，時雜以俚語韻語及外國語法。縱筆所至
不檢束，學者競效之，號為新文體。老輩則痛
恨，詆為野狐。然其文條理明晰，筆鋒常帶情
感，對於讀者，別有一種魔力焉。(*zhuanji* v.34
62)

Liang Qichao's effort to "create a more accessible style
that incorporated vernacular elements" (*Huters* 248) was
not only aimed at literary renovation but also charged
with political commitment. As part of this effort, Liang
actively promoted political fiction by elevating the status
of fiction in the Chinese literary system and by translating
and composing novels. As Qian Xuantong (1887-1939),
one of the most active participants in the New Literature
Movement, accurately remarks, "Liang Rengong [Qichao]
was actually the first person of the new literature ......
his genius and vision can be found in his introduction of
Japan's new literature, use of new terms and colloquialisms
in writing, and elevation of drama and fiction to match the
status of essay" (*Qian* 3). In the following sections, I first
discuss Liang Qichao's reinterpretation of the concept of
novel, a radical move owing to Japanese influence. Then
I analyze the development of Liang's understanding of
fiction and its relations with politics by investigating the
translation strategies employed in two of his translations
of Shiba Shiro and Jules Verne. Finally, I focus on Liang
Qichao's contribution to the establishment of a standardized Chinese language and modern literature.

Xiao shuo, *Shōsetsu*, **and Fiction**

Liang Qichao has been known for his active introduction of Japanese translations of Western terms in his
works and credited for popularizing many such terms in
China. However, what interests us most is the question of

whether or not there was a kind of mechanism responsible for Liang Qichao's choice of translated terms. Evidence indicates that Liang did not passively borrow an established translated term from a Japanese book for the convenience of his own writing. Rather, he always took into consideration factors such as accuracy of translation, context, and audience before he finally used a foreign term. The linguistic problem notwithstanding, his decision-making process implicitly involved a transformation of discourse and epistemology in Chinese culture caused by the impact of Western knowledge.

Liang Qichao's concern for his audience can be demonstrated by his switch from Yan Fu's translation of "evolution" as *tian yan* to the Japanese translation *shinka*. As I have explained in the last chapter, tian literally means "nature" or "heaven," *yan* "evolvement". So *tian yan*, literally meaning "natural evolvement," is an excellent translation of Huxley's concept of "evolution" as "the historical development of a biological group (as a race or species)." By this translation, Yan Fu tones down the sense of progressive development imbedded in the concept of evolution, "a process of continuous change from a lower, simpler, or worse to a higher, more complex, or better state." Rather, Yan Fu focuses on the combative nature of life and the hardship of existence.

The Japanese translation, however, foregrounds the meaning of "evolution" as "a process of change in a certain direction." The introduction of evolutionism into Japan was generally attributed to Edward Sylvester Morse (1838-1925), an American zoologist and orientalist. Morse was invited to lecture on zoology, archeology, and anthropology at Tokyo University from 1877 to 1880. The word "evolution" in his lectures was translated in several Japanese words which all had the connotation of "development." It was Inoue Tetsujirō (1855-1944) who coined the

105

term *shinka* as the translation of "evolution" in his 1881 *Tetsugaku jii* (A Dictionary of Philosophy). Inoue Tetsujirō was famous for both his introduction of Western philosophy into Japan and his study of Chinese philosophy with the help of Western philosophical thinking. His authority in philosophy and social science circles assured the popular acceptance of the term *shinka*, which had became the only Japanese translation of "evolution" when Liang Qichao went to Japan. In Chinese, *shinka* is pronounced as *jin hua*, in which *jin* means "advance" while *hua* means "transformation." The Japanese term conveys explicitly the meaning of progress. Actually, Yan Fu was among the first to use jin hua in the Chinese context. Upon the request of Wu Rulun, Yan Fu added titles to every section of his translation. The title of his last section of *Tian yan lun (Evolution and Ethics)* was named *jin hua*. The corresponding text in Huxley's work discusses the relation between evolution and ethics by arguing "the ethical progress of society depends, not on imitating the cosmic process, still less in running away from it, but in combating it" (83). Because the word "evolution" appears only once in this part, which is translated as *tian yan*, we have reason to question the title *"jin hua"* as a translation of "evolution." It is still unclear how Yan Fu got to know the word *jin hua* and why he used this term only once in his translation.

Liang Qichao acclaimed Yan Fu's translation of *Evolution and Ethics* and propagated avidly the idea of evolution to the Chinese people. In his writing, Yan Fu's term *tian yan* was his only choice in terms of evolution until late 1902 when he abandoned Yan Fu's term and switched to *jin hua*. After a four-year stay in Japan, Liang Qichao had been exposed to various Japanese ideas and was familiar with a range of Japanese concepts. Compared to *yan hua*, the obvious connotation of progress in *jin hua* would be better for arousing the sense of urgency in Chinese readers.

To emphasize this sense of urgency at the time when the 1901 Boxer Protocol marked a new high of the imperialist colonization of China, Liang Qichao adopted the Japanese translation which took root and has flourished in China ever since.

Liang Qichao's inconsistent use of the Chinese term *sheng ji xue* 生計學 and the Japanese term *jing ji xue* (*keizaigaku*) as the translation of "political economy" or "economics" reflects his compromise between the accuracy of translation and his audience. Liang Qichao's search for the right translation of the English term lasted almost 20 years. His first use of a translation for "economics" appeared in his 1877 essay "Bian fa tong yi" (A General Discussion of Reform): "Among them, books of economics (*fu guo xue*), which the Japanese call *keizaigaku*, all accord with the popular sentiments and products of the many countries of the world, waxing and waning according to circumstances" (*wenji* v.1 71). While Liang Qichao noted the Japanese translation, he decided to use a Chinese term coined by the *Tong wen guan* (Interpreters College), the first institution established in 1862 in China for the study of Western languages. The term *fu guo xue* 富國學, literally meaning "theory of enriching the nation," was also used by other open-minded scholars such as Zheng Guanying (1841-1923). In another essay "Shi ji huo zhi lie zhuan jin yi" (The contemporary meaning of the biographies of economists in the Records of the Grand Historian), which was published in the same year, he wrote, "Western scholars have discussed economics (*fu guo xue*), and their debates have proliferated and become extremely detailed...Thus, scholars of economics (*li cai zhi xue*) note that there are no differences between countries" (*wenji* v.2 42). While Liang still used *fu guo xue*, he introduced a four-character compound *li cai zhi xue* 理財之學, literally meaning "theory of managing wealth."

In his translation of Adam Smith's *Inquiry into the Nature and Causes of the Wealth of Nations*, which was published in 1902 under the Chinese title *Yuan fu* (Trace the origin of wealth), Yan Fu used *sheng ji* 生計 as the translation of "economics" because he thought *li cai* was too narrow while the Japanese term was too broad. In his review of Yan Fu's translation, Liang Qichao made his observations: "For the English term 'political economy,' we have yet to establish a Chinese term. The Japanese translate it as *keizaigaku*, but this is still unstable. Mr. Yan would like to use the term *sheng ji*, but it, too, is still not widely adopted. For the time being, we shall have to plan for a truly worthy term in our language that contains the senses of both politics and the economy" (*wenji* v.7 98).

In his study of Liang Qichao's translations of "political economy," Mori Tokihito gives us a detailed description of Liang Qichao's uses of different translations in various occasions over the years. In summary, Mori Tokihito concludes that Liang's choice of the term depended on:

> who the target audience was and what the goal of using the term at the time was. Liang Qichao's personal choice, the one with which he felt most comfortable, was the term *shengji*, but in the period of radical change in Chinese society at the time of the 1911 Revolution, the term *jingji* had already claimed substantial adherents. If he wished to continue his dialogue with Chinese society in these circumstances, Liang had no choice but to use the term *jingji* even though he was personally opposed to it. (37-8)

Though Liang Qichao was concerned more about his readers and accuracy of translation in his selections of appropriate translations for "evolution" and "economy," political considerations definitely played a role since he realized that translation was not only a matter of wording but also of conveying epistemological differences. His promotion of *xiao shuo* or fiction represents the most successful endeavor Liang Qichao made to change Chinese culture. *Xiao shuo* is the Chinese translation of "fiction" while *Shōsetsu* is the Japanese translation. The Chinese word *xiao shuo* (small talk) first appeared in the great philosophical text *Zhuangzi*, meaning "rumor", "anecdote," and "trivial story," as opposed to Zhuang Zi's another term *da da*, meaning "great understanding." Zhuang Zi's derogatory use of this word emphasizes the negative quality of a non-literary discourse when it jeopardizes qualities of beauty and the sublime in an article. It was not until the Han Dynasty that *xiao shuo* began to gain the connotation of literary genre. In his political book Xin lun "New Discussions," Huan Tan (c.24 BCE-56 AD), a famous early Han musician and scholar, argues that xiao shuo is worth reading because this kind of short writing expresses one's political and social views by piecing together many small speeches. Unlike Zhuang Zi, Huan Tan interprets the smallness inherent in the word *xiao shuo* in terms of quantity by foregrounding the literary quality of brevity. As a Confucian critic, he also furnishes xiao shuo with a didactic aim as a tool for "governing the self and managing the family." In *Han shu Yi wen zhi* (Annotated Bibliography of Literature of the History of the Han Dynasty), Ban Gu (32-92 AD), one of the great Chinese historians, lists *xiao shuo* as one of the ten different philosophical schools since the pre-Qin era. According to Ban Gu's characterization, the creators of xiao shuo may "grow out of officials of lower status and are makers of street talk and alley gossip by engaging themselves in conversations along the roads and walkways" (157). To justify the existence of *xiao shuo*, Ban Gu turns to the teaching of Confucius*. He quotes the words of the master as follows:

---

* The passage Ban Gu quoted was actually the words of Zixia (c. 507-420 BC), one of Confucius's famous disciples and a distinguished educator of the Spring and Autumn period.

Confucius said: "Even in inferior studies and emp-loyments there is something worth being looked at; but if it be attempted to carry them out to what is re-mote, there is a danger of their proving inapplicable." Therefore, the superior man neither practices them nor forbids them. The person who has street-smart records what he sees as a reminder. Even he records something, they are only the words of woodmen and madmen.

孔子曰："雖小道，必有可觀者焉，致遠恐泥，是以君子弗為也。"然亦弗滅也。閭裡小知者之所及，亦使綴而不忘。如或一言可採，此亦芻蕘狂夫之議也。(157)

Ban Gu's account of the origin of *xiao shuo* points out that *xiao shuo* is a record of common people's life. Comparing historical records that document significant historical events and figures by official historians, *xiao shuo* is charac-terized by its shortness in form and the anecdotical nature of its content. On the one hand, Confucian scholars ac-knowledge its effectiveness in understanding public opin-ion and social psychology. On the other hand, *xiao shuo* is viewed as "inferior" and unreliable. Most works listed un-der the title *xiao shuo* by Ban Gu are myths, legends, tales, and fables. In his book *Zhongguo xiao shuo shi lue* (A Concise History of Chinese Fiction), Lu Xun asserts that *xiao shuo* in Ban Gu's category is "similar to the concept of fiction in our time" (5). The anecdotal quality of *xiao shuo* was extended to fantasy when *xiao shuo* writers started to de-velop a consciousness of form in the Six Dynasties and Jin Dynasty. The most popular genre was called *zhi guai xiao shuo* 志怪小说 (recording the abnormal). Characters in *zhi guai xiao shuo* were usually ghosts, fox-spirits, forebodings, dreams of premonition, metamorphoses, fortune-tellers, magical objects, and the like. Stories were always about the cohabitation of human and supernatural powers or figures.

Treating the underworld as something true, writers tried to express their understanding of the unity of time, space, and character, and their poised attitude toward the blurring borderline between life and death, between fantasy and reality (see *Wang*, 1984). Tang *xiao shuo* writers preferred to write about romance and marked their achievements in the genre *chuan qi* 传奇 (conveying the marvelous). The biggest difference between *chuan qi* and *zhi guai* was that *chuan qi* writers intentionally made up stories to convey their emotional responses to marvelous romances. These writers consciously kept a distance from the writing conventions of history and appreciated imagery as an indispensable aesthetic quality of *xiao shuo*.

With the rise of vernacular fiction in the Song Dynasty, which was written in spoken Chinese, those styles of *xiao shuo* which were written in classical Chinese were categorized as classical fiction. Later generations of Chinese literati took it as a literary convention that classical fiction should be a short story about supernatural figures and irregular incidents. *Liao zhai zhi yi* (Strange Stories from a Chinese Studio), written by early Qing writer Pu Songling (1640-1715), was regarded as one of the most successful classical fictions. It is actually a collection of short stories about ghosts, fox-spirits, and forebodings. Lin Shu also wrote some classical novels attacking advocates of vernacular Chinese and literary revolution in the 1910s. Though classical *xiao shuo* writers often incorporated moralism based on Confucian ideas, its conventional subject matters were usually opposed to the teaching of Confucius that "The subjects on which the Master did not talk were extraordinary things, feats of strength, disorder, and spiritual beings" (Ruan 2483). Therefore, classical *xiao shuo* has been regarded as a tool for literati to fulfill their desire for fantasy and has circulated within small literati circles because of its dependence on classical Chinese.

Vernacular fiction, however, took root in the storytelling tradition and gained popular acceptance by entertaining illiterate and low-educated people with mostly historical stories. With the concentration of population and wealth in several cities during the Song Dynasty, city life became more and more colorful and *shuo hua* (telling stories) emerged as a popular entertainment in city life. Storytelling took place at the temple fairs, teahouses, wineshops, and other entertainment areas. Storytellers practiced their performance both in spoken and singing forms. According to *Dongjing meng hua lu*, the themes of story-telling contained *jiangshi* 讲史 (expounding history), *xiaoshuo* 小说 (adventure), *shuo hunhua* 说诨话, *shuo san fen* 说三分 (telling about Three Kingdoms), *wu dai shi* 五代史 (telling about Five Dynasties) (Meng 40). The scripts of storytelling are generally recognized as the origin of vernacular fiction. In the development of vernacular fiction, *Yan yi* 演义 (expounding history) and *ping hua* 平话 (telling stories) were the two most popular synonyms of fiction. These two terms also betray two characteristics of vernacular fiction. *Yan yi* defines the subject matter and the function of fiction: historical events and figures are always the favorite topics for fiction writers who customarily bring out moral meanings and historical wisdom from history. *Ping hua* leaves a deep mark on techniques, skills, and structure of the vernacular novel: because *ping hua* originated from storytelling which by nature implies a face-to-face immediacy between a storyteller and his audience, formalities used to attend to listeners remained in the vernacular novel. A vernacular fiction usually starts with narrator's calling for attention from readers and ends with a cliché "If you audience want to know what happened next, please wait for the next chapter." A couplet title is always given to each chapter indicating the plotline in the chapter. Poems are used to portray characters' appearance, clothes, and personality and to describe settings around the characters. Because the subject and literary formality of vernacular fiction tended to cater to the taste of ill-educated people, such novels were always placed on the margin of the system of Chinese literature before the twentieth century (see *Hanan*, 1981; *Rolston*, 1997; *Hsia*, 1968).

When the Chinese first came in contact with Western fiction, they did not immediately establish a connection between fiction and *xiao shuo*, partly because *xiao shuo* had not become the nomenclature designating the literary genre in the modern sense. It was through the Japanese translation of the term "fiction" that the Chinese tradition of *xiao shuo* was successfully absorbed into Western discourse of fiction and literature. Liang Qichao was the person who contributed most to the acceptance of *xiao shuo* as nomenclature and to the successful transformation. The Japanese term *shōsetsu*, literally meaning "small talk," is in fact the translation of the Chinese term *xiao shuo*. In his 1885 book *Shōsetsu Shinzui* (The Essence of Fiction), Tsubouchi Shoyo (1859-1935), a famous Japanese critic and translator, chose *shōsetsu* to translate the Western concept of fiction and expressed his literary idea of "art for art's sake." Japanese political fiction writers held an entirely different view of the function of fiction, but they also used the term *shōsetsu* to refer to fiction as a literary genre. Before the term *shōsetsu* was retranslated back to China, Chinese scholars tended to use the term *shuo bu* (Category of storytelling) to designate Western fiction and Chinese works under its influence. In his 1896 reform proposal sent to the emperor "Bian fa tong yi" (General principles of reforms), Liang Qichao devoted a section to *shuo bu* arguing the uselessness of the traditional Chinese fiction and calling for using vernacular Chinese to compose a new kind of genre. In explaining why their newspaper would open a section for fiction, Yan Fu and Xia Zengyou in 1897 wrote a lengthy editorial in *Guo wen bao (National News)* and also used the term *shuo bu* for fiction. Not until 1898 when Liang Qichao published his influential paper "Yi yin zheng zhi xiao shuo xu" ("On translating and publishing political fiction") was the term *xiao shuo* connected to fiction. Liang Qichao's use of *xiao shuo* was not only an act of translation, but also a promotion of fiction as a genre and of Western discourses.

In his 1902 essay "Lun xiao shuo yu qun zhi zhi guan xi" (On the Relationship Between Fiction and the Education of the Masses), Liang Qichao was the first advocate for fiction in the history of Chinese literary criticism. He contends with a passionate and aggressive manner that, "to educate the people of a nation, to reshape their morale, we must have new fiction; to reform religion and politics, we must have new fiction; to change their customs and let them learn new crafts, we must have new fiction; to remould their ideology and their character, we must have new fiction" (*zhuanji* v.10 127). Fiction, according to Liang, is no longer a vulgar form of amusement, but the spirit of the nation. However, Liang gave traditional Chinese fiction a very low score by stating that Chinese fiction did nothing but corrupt and degrade the moral behavior of readers.

Liang's political agenda led to a discrepancy between his unprecedented promotion of fiction as a primary literary form and his criticism and denunciation of Chinese fiction. Facing the national, cultural, and political crisis of China in the second half of the nineteenth century, Liang the reformer tried to seek a less violent way for China to achieve its modern transition. Like most his exceptional contemporaries, he foregrounded the part played by culture and ideas in the social transformation, a necessary conclusion drawn from the Confucian treatment of literature as a moral tool. According to Confucian literary critics, literature is the vehicle to propagate moral principles endorsed by saints; literary aesthetics function as a promoter of the acceptance of ideas. The popularity of fiction among the majority Chinese suggested it as the most efficient way for Liang to educate the masses. To demonstrate this efficiency of fiction's impact on readers, Liang theorized the function of fiction as the power of influence, of catharsis, of stimulation, and of distilling. By these powers, fiction attracts more people to stories for amusement whose moral standard is allegedly much lower than that found in poetry and prose.

Liang's promotion of fiction was also determined by the fact that audiences of fiction were mainly illiterates to whom Liang Qichao wanted to bring enlightenment. Though Yan Fu's and Lin shu's works exerted tremendous influence in China, their targeted audience consisted of Chinese intellectuals. Their works were written in classical Chinese, a form of Chinese used and understood only by literati. However, because Liang placed the future of China on the shoulders of educated masses, he concentrated his attention on transforming traditional Chinese fiction to new fiction by inserting new moral and political content.

Although Liang's proposition of fiction as the most important literary genre was very radical, acceptance of this idea was unbelievably smooth and quick. Liang's rhetoric of persuasion was to use foreign examples to legitimate this idea. Based on some basic but often inaccurate knowledge of Western fiction, Liang made many false generalizations about Western fiction to sustain his political propositions. One of these generalizations was that political fiction is the most popular fiction in the West. To validate his point, Liang translated a Japanese political novel and wrote an unfinished political novel entitled Xin Zhongguou wei lai ji (The Future of New China). However inaccurate his observation was, most Chinese were not able to check it; the popular belief of the superiority of the West helped Liang's promotion of new fiction.

Translation and Political Fiction

Liang Qichao first came into contact with political fiction when he took refuge in Japan after the bloody crackdown of the Hundred Days' Reform in September 1898. On a Japanese warship which was arranged for him to flee to Japan, the captain gave Liang a copy of *Kajin no kigu* (Unexpected Encounters with Beautiful Women) as an amusement for the long journey. Written by Shiba Shiro (1852-1922), a.k.a. Tokai Sanshi (Wandering Literati from the Eastern Sea), *Kajin no kigu* was one of the most successful and popular political novels in Meiji Japan. According to H.A.L. Fisher's definition, political fiction is the novel which "chiefly concerns itself with men and women engaged in contemporary political life and discussing contemporary political ideas" (*Harvie* 2). It is generally held that political fiction emerged in the 1840s in England when Benjamin Disraeli wrote the trilogy of *Coningsby*, *Sybil*, and *Tancred* in 1844-1847, in the hope of expounding his political ideas. In his book *The Political Novel* (1924), Morris Edmund Speare distinguishes the political novel as a unique genre and maps its scope through its relationship with British nationalism. In Speare's opinion, novels by Disraeli, Anthony Trollope, and George Meredith serve as examples of political novels because they deal with the operations of state apparatuses.

The introduction of the political novel into Japan started in the 1880s when Japanese intellectuals demanded political freedom and people's rights from their Emperor. In her survey of the political novel in the Meiji era, Hiroko Willcock remarks, "The Meiji political novel became a medium to promote the political ideology of the author as well as the political party to which the author belonged. It was to serve the reading public with knowledge of new ideas and a vision of an advanced, modern society" (*Willcock* 2). Translations of Western novels, such as *Ernest Maltravers* (1878), *Pilgrim's*

Progress (1880), and *Coningsby* (1884), helped fiction to become a legitimate form of literary genre. Western political consciousness and scientific spirit came to Japan hand in hand with Western literature. Traditional Chinese culture gradually lost its influence on Japanese literature. In March 1883, Yano Ryukei published the first part of *Keikoku bidan* (Illustrious Tales of Statesmanship), an immediate hit that ushered in the prime time of the political novel in Japan. Yano was very active in political activities and became one of the leaders of the Reform Party. In his preface, he proposes his ideal fiction: "The goal of fiction writers is not to play with exquisite devices or to describe customs and human emotions; it is to demonstrate opinions and principles and to smoothly shape people's views – in other words, the goal lies outside the text" (*Willcock* 5). Intended to write a historical work about his ideal society, Yano turned it to a novel because of the shortage of historical materials. In *Keikoku bidan* he depicted a utopian society where Confucian democracy was practiced and popular rights and national rights were secured.

If *Keikoku bidan* represents the political novels written by Japanese politicians, Shiba Shiro's *Kajin no kigu* (Unexpected Encounters with Beautiful Women) is the most representative novel of another kind of political novel. According to Horace Z. Feldman, the feature of this kind of political novel is that they are "filled with romantic fervor and patriotic indignation and bursting with national pride, but not directly focused on the Japanese political scene" (Feldman 248). Before he went to study in America in 1879, Shiba Shiro studied in Tokyo at a private academy for the children of former samurai. During the six years in America, Shiba Shiro studied at several schools and finally received a bachelor of Finance degree from the Wharton School. After he went back to Japan, he published the first two volumes of *Kajin no kigu* in 1885. He spent twelve years completing all eight volumes and the last volume came out in 1897.

The novel tells the stories of four nationalists from Japan, China, Spain, and Ireland. When the Japanese student Tokai Sanshi visits the Liberty Bell in Philadelphia, he runs into two girls, Youlan from Spain and Honglian from Ireland. Youlan's father is the Spanish general who is fighting for the establishment of a parliamentary system, while Honglian's father has died in the battle against the British King. The two girls take refuge in America and hide in the place of Ding Tailian, whose ancestors left China after the Ming Dynasty was taken over by the Qing Dynasty. Ding's father was killed in the Opium war with the British. After they become friends at the meeting in Philadelphia, the four depart and participate in revolutionary activities in different places, including Korea, Spain, Ireland, Poland, Italy, Turkey, and Egypt. The narration of political events around the world is interspersed with the romance between Sanshi and Youlan. At last, their romance does not work out because of interruptions and Sanshi decides to go around the world with a government delegation. *Kajin no kigu* contains many items of autobiographical information and expresses Shiba Shiro's particular views on Japan's problems and world politics.

The first installment of Liang Qichao's translation of *Kajin no kigu* was published in the first issue of *Qing yi bao* (Topics of the Day) in December 1898 under the title *Jia ren qi yu* 佳人奇遇. *Qing yi bao* was edited by Liang Qichao in Yokohama and was one of the most outspoken reformist newspapers. Shiba Shiro was listed as the author of the original novel, while no translator's name was given. Liang Qichao claimed he was the translator in a poem. And when the translation was published in book form in 1901, Liang Qichao was credited as translator. In "Editor's Note" attached to Liang Qichao's translation of *Kajin no kigu* in his collected works, the editor narrated the translation process: "Mr. Rengong [Liang Qichao] took refuge in 1898 and went to Japan. [He] translated the book on the ship for entertainment and did not leave his name on it. His translation has been out of print for a long time" (*zhuanji* v.10 1). In Liang Qichao's first biography, his biographer Ding Wenjiang (1887-1936) also recorded this event: "In August of the year Wuxu [October 1898], Mr. Liang escaped from the arrest and went to Japan. He had no personal belongings on this Japanese warship. The captain presented him a *Kajin no kigu* (Unexpected Encounters with Beautiful Women). Mr. Liang translated it while reading it, then published in the *Qing yi bao*. The beginning of translation started on the warship" (*Ding* 31).

Despite such an account, some scholars have taken issue because they question Liang Qichao's ability in the Japanese language. In his paper on the contribution of Yan Fu and Liang Qichao to New Fiction, C. T. Hsia casts his doubt, "since he [Liang Qichao] did not seriously study the language until after his arrival in Japan, one may well wonder if he knew enough Japanese at the time to translate the work even though its style was highly Sinicized" (235). Liang Qichao admitted that he started to learn Japanese only after he arrived in Japan. In his *San shi zi zhu* (Autobiography at the Age of Thirty), Liang Qichao recorded that he had discussed with his like-minded friends establishing a newspaper after he arrived in Japan in October 1898: "since I stayed in Tokyo, Japan, for one year, I became able to read some Japanese and my thought changed drastically" (*wenji* v.11 8). If Liang Qichao could only read "some Japanese" one year later, how would he be able to translate Shiba Shiro's novel when he read the book on the ship in 1898? This question has led the Japanese scholar Yamada Keizo to the speculation that someone else translated the novel. Yamada Keizo argues that this someone was Luo Pu, a progressive student who studied in Japan at that time (*Yamada* 390). Both Luo Pu and Liang Qichao were students of Kang Youwei. Luo Pu went to study in Japan before Liang; therefore, he had a better knowledge of Japanese. Luo Pu also worked with Liang Qichao in 1902 in translating Jules Verne's *Deux ans de vacances* via Morita Shiken's Japanese translation. The most convincing evidence of Yamada Keizo's claim comes from a story by Feng Ziyou. In "Xin hai ge min qian hai nei wai ge ming shu bao yi lan" ("Reviews of revolutionary newspapers and magazines before the 1911 Revolution"), Feng Ziyou says the following about Luo Pu: "This novel [*Kajin no kigu*] describes fighters of colonized nations in the West and America and nationless Chinese striving to recover their countries. It was written by a Japanese writer Shiba Shiro and translated by Pu Luo. The translation was serialized in *Qing yi bao*" (113). After he presents his argument, Yamada Keizo believes that Liang Qichao is not the translator of *Kajin no kigu* and it is "more accurate to view him as the introducer of the novel" (*Yamada* 398).

Though the suspicion of C. T. Hsia and Yamada Keizo is warranted, we cannot simply rule out the possibility that Liang Qichao did indeed translate the novel. Contrary to C. T. Hsia's conclusion, many scholars think the "highly sinicized" style of the original helped Liang Qichao's understanding of the novel. In his introduction to Japanese literature, Donald Keene comes to the conclusion that "It could not have been very difficult for the distinguished scholar Liang Ch'i-ch'ao [Qichao] to make the Chinese translation of this work!" (*Keene* 85). Because after examining the Japanese novel, he asserts, "The language [of *Kajin no kigu*] is ornate, difficult, and exceedingly conventional, borrowing heavily form the stereotypes of Chinese fiction. The characters, regardless of their country, are constantly referring to events in Chinese history, using all the appropriate clichés" (*Keene* 85-86). Aiming at remedying the scholarly neglect of the Japanese political novel of the mid Meiji period, Sakaki Atsuko takes *Kajin no kigu* as an example for exploring "some of the implications of the shifting reputation of the political novel." (Sakaki 84) She determines that many Japanese writers of political novel were trained under the heavy influence of traditional Chinese culture. On the writing style of *Kajin no kigu*, Sakaki says:

> It is written entirely – including conversations among the characters – in *kanbun kakikudashi tai*. It uses classical and literary diction throughout rather than incorporating modern or conversational language in some passages, such as dialogue. Apart from maintaining the traditional linguistic conventions of *kanbun kakikudashi tai*, the author adhered to a sinicized mode of presentation. The text is printed in the mixture of kanji and katakana common in premodern Japanese representation of Chinese poetry and prose rather than the combination of kanji and hiragana used typically in the modern colloquial shosetsu. (*Sakaki* 92)

My own personal reading experience has also demonstrated that the original was understandable to a Chinese without knowledge of Japanese, though it was not a pleasant experience. I juxtapose below the first passage of the original and Liang Qichao's translation below as a demonstration.

Original:

東海散士一日費府ノ擲立閣ニ登リ仰テ自由ノ破
鐘　（歐米ノ民大事撞テ之ヲ報ズ. 始メ米國ノ擲立
スルニ當テ吉凶必ズ閣上アル毎ニ鐘デノ鐘ヲ撞ク
。 鐘遂ニ裂ク。 後人呼テ自由ノ破鐘ト云フ）ヲ
觀、俯テ擲立ノ遺文ヲ讀ミ、當時米人ノ義旗ヲ舉
テ英王ノ虐政ヲ除キ、卒ニ能ク　擲立ク自主ノ民
タルノ高風ヲ追懷シ、俯仰感慨ニ堪ヘズ。 愀然ト

シテ窓ニ倚テ眺臨ス。會て二姫アリ。階ヲ繞テ登リ來ル。翠羅面ヲ覆ヒ、暗影疎香白羽ノ春冠ヲ戴キ、輕縠ノ短羅ヲ衣、文華ノ長裾ヲ曳キ、風雅高表實ニ人ヲ驚カス。一小亭ヲ指シ相語テ曰ク、那ノ處ハ卽チ是レ一千七百七十四年、十三州ノ名士始メテ相曾シ、國家前途ノ國是ヲ計畫センシ處ナリト。

Translation:

東海散士一日登費府獨立閣仰觀自由之破鐘俯讀獨立之遺愾然怀想當時米人舉義旗除英苛法卒能獨立為自由之民倚窗臨眺迫怀高風俯仰感慨俄而見二妃繞階來登翠羅覆面暗影疏香戴白羽之春冠衣輕之短裙羅曳文華之長裙風雅高表飴盡精目相与指一小亭而語曰那處即是一千七百七十四年十三州之名士第一次會議國是之處也

It is obvious that Liang kept almost all the Chinese characters of the original in his translation. Though difficult to connect broken phrases for someone like me who does not understand Japanese, it was not hard to recapture the basic content and plot of the novel. What Liang Qichao did was to make some changes to the order of words to make his translation Chinese.* Judging from the fluency of the translation, it was very likely that someone who understood Japanese polished Liang's translation or even did a sort of oral rendition for Liang.

Because Shiba Shiro used "classical and literary diction" and borrowed "stereotypes" and "clichés" of classical

---

* This was not the unusual way for Chinese writers to translate Japanese works in the early twentieth century. Bao Tianxiao (1875-1973), a writer and a translator of Japanese literature, admitted that the reason he chose to translate Japanese works was because Japanese works were full of Chinese characters. When he started to translate, he had no knowledge of Japanese. However, his translations were popular at the time.

Chinese, Liang Qichao translated the book in classical Chinese against the principles of plain language he had proposed. His little knowledge of Japanese definitely left him no choice but to copy the original classical Chinese expressions. As a convention for vernacular fiction, the title of each chapter needed to be a couplet which indicates the plot of the chapter. In Liang Qichao's creation of his own novels and other translations, this convention was strictly observed. The exception in this first translation was not because he respected the rule of loyalty to the original and tried to practice the strategy of literal translation. We have seen from my previous discussions, when Lin Shu rewrote the oral translation in his highly stylistic classical Chinese, he had aesthetic, moral, and marketability considerations in mind; Yan Fu's choice of classical Chinese as his language to translate was not without political and aesthetic calculus. On the contrary, Liang Qichao used classical Chinese in this translation partly because he had to take advantage of classical Chinese expressions in the original. Liang Qichao devotes all the pages of his "Translator's Preface" to introduce the idea of political fiction, but provides his readers with little information about the author and the book itself. He does not bother to mention the classical Chinese literary characteristics of the original and says nothing about his translation strategy. The most important reason may be that Liang Qichao hadn't found an appropriate style that was both agreeable with his political ideas and persuasive to his readers. The urgent call for this new writing style was finally answered by Liang Qichao a few years later after he had absorbed Japanese ideas and language. The newness of his ideas and style will be discussed later when we examine his translation of Morita Shiken's translation of the English version of Jules Verne's *Deux ans de vacances*.

Besides his choice of language in translation, Liang Qichao practiced a common translation strategy used by his contemporary translators Lin Shu and Yan Fu, namely that of deletion. Compared with Lin Shu, Liang Qichao's translation shows greater loyalty to the original content. However, he has deleted all the poems, prefaces, and author's notes in the original. Liang's decision to delete notes and prefaces was not due to a language problem, because many of them were written in Chinese. In notes and prefaces, Shiba Shiro usually introduced his personal experiences, publishing information and the receptions of his novel. Liang Qichao deleted them because they were irrelevant to the novel. In the original, the author added many reviews from his friends. These reviews were not translated, though many of them gave insights into Shiba Shiro in particular and the political novel in general.

One year after he had translated *Kajin no kigu*, Liang Qichao uttered his understanding of the political novel:

> The novel was one of the factors that contributed greatly to the Japanese restoration. Between 1885 and 1886, calls for liberty and people's rights were sounded loudly in Japan. Therefore, Western fictions regarding French and Roman revolutions were translated one by one...... In the face of the boom of translation, creations of political fiction were on the rise. The writers were all great statesmen. They declared their political views through their characters in the books. That is why we can read them only as a novel. The most powerful works in indoctrinating the minds of Japanese people were *Kajin no kigu* and *Keikoku bidan* (*zhuanji* v.9 31).

At the time when Liang Qichao translated *Kajin no kigu*, the political novel was no longer a popular literary genre in Japan while science fiction had become a new tool to introduce Western ideas. Liang Qichao was keenly aware of this trend and made efforts to create a new writing style to accommodate this new genre and new ideas.

Translating Newness in Science Fiction

The introduction of science fiction into Japan started with the translation of Jules Verne. Kawashima Chúnosuke's translation of *Le Tour du monde en quatre-vingts jours* in 1878 was the first Japanese translation of Jules Verne. After the political novel lost its appeal to Japanese readers in the late 1880s, translations of science fiction provided Japanese intellectuals with alternative ways to fulfill their political desires and aesthetic imagination. In his paper "Japanese Utopian Literature from the 1870s to the Present and the Influence of Western Utopianism," Yoriko Moichi gives us a brief account of Japanese utopian/dystopian literature from the 1870s and states that Japanese writers "have modeled their utopian writings under the influence of Western utopian literature. Japan's first introduction of Western concepts of utopia in the Meiji Restoration was only for the purpose of political ideology, and utopia as a literary genre could not be consolidated at this time" (*Moichi* 95).

Among translators of science fiction in the Meiji era, Morita Shiken (1861-1897) was the most famous and prolific one. Well-versed in traditional Chinese literature and culture, Morita was known in his translations for his elegant and stylish Japanese. During his short life, he translated more than 10 science novels mainly by Jules Verne. His translation of *Deux ans de vacances*, first serialized in the magazine *Shonen Sekai (Children's world)* from May to August 1876, was the most popular translation of his and became a classic book for children in Japan. Jules Verne's *Deux ans de vacances* was published in 1888. It tells of a group of schoolboys who plan to spend a six-week vacation in Auckland, New Zealand. However, the ship they board is caught by a storm and the children are cast away in an uncharted island. In the next two years, they manage to survive on the island with their struggles to overcome adversities. After being taken over by pirates, they finally overpower the pirates and secure the pirates' ship to escape. The idea of "struggle for existence" is clearly stated in the novel, and the author tries to build up children's minds with respect to bravery and the adventurous spirit.

Besides these Japanese translations, reading Jules Verne and science fiction in Chinese was not completely new to Liang Qichao. In 1900, Xue Shaohui (1866-1911) had translated *Le Tour du monde en quatre-vingts jours* through the English version by M. Towel and N. D. Anvers. This translation into Chinese was the first translation *per se* of science fiction and of Jules Verne.* The book was so successful that translation of science fiction became popular. In 1902 *Vingt mille lieues sous les mers* was translated into Chinese before Liang started to translate *Deux ans de vacances* in the same year. After he had stayed in Japan for 4 years, Liang Qichao's Japanese improved rapidly and he was able to read Japanese books in Japanese.

Comparing it with Western languages, Liang Qichao regarded Japanese as the best tool for acquiring new knowledge in that Japanese was much easier to learn. He admitted that he felt comfortable with the Japanese language after only half a year in Japan. He went to school to learn Japanese and was very active in social activities with Japanese friends. If he had translated *Kajin no kigu* thanks largely to the heavy use of classic Chinese, his Japanese now was good enough to allow him to translate a modern Japanese book.

In addition to the improvement of language ability, Liang Qichao came in contact with a variety of Western

---

* In 1891, Timothy Richard (1845-1919) wrote a story in Chinese based on Edward Bellamy's *Looking Backward: 2000-1887*. His work was first serialized in an English newspaper *The Global Magazine* under the title *hui tou kan ji lue (Looking back)*. In 1894, his translation was published in book form under the new title *Bai nian yi jiao (A sleep of one hundred years)*. Interestingly, Timothy did not tell his readers his work was a translation.

and Japanese opinions that shaped his political attitude and way of thinking. During his stay in Japan, on the one hand, he edited two Chinese newspapers and kept direct connections with intellectuals in China. On the other hand, he socialized with many important Japanese intellectuals such as Fukuzawa Yukichi (1835-1901) and was influenced by the Japanese interpretation of Confucianism. In his article "Lun xue Riben wen zhi yi" ("On the benefits of learning Japanese"), he described his excitement in reading Japanese books: "I have been in Japan for several months. I studied the Japanese language and read Japanese books. There were so many books that I had not heard of. [After reading,] the ideas that I had not understood rushed in my mind; it was like sunshine coming in a dark room, and like wine pouring into a thirsty stomach" (*wenji* v.4 80). In the meantime, ideas of nationalism, anarchism, and parliamentarism flourished in the mid-Meiji Japan. Liang Qichao was particularly attracted to nationalism. In a 1902 letter to his mentor Kang Youwei, Liang Qichao introduced to Kang ideas of nationalism: "We are in the prime time of nationalism: a nation cannot be established without it. I swear to promote it with my mouth and my pen forever. The reason that I awaken the spirit of our nation is to overturn the Manchu power…the fate of the Qing government is sealed. We expected the power to return to the Emperor, what did we get?" (*wenji* v.3 12). Liang Qichao had been the most avid reformer only four years earlier, but one Japanese book had changed his ideas completely.

Thanks to Yan Fu's masterful interpretation of Huxley's ideas, Liang Qichao was still a believer of evolutionism. However, he began to look at it through an epistemological binary between the West and East. His brief visit to Hawaii in 1902 gave him a chance to experience personally Western culture and to reflect on Chinese culture through foreign eyes. In his groundbreaking book *Orientalism*,

Edward Said criticizes the Western way of thinking that is "based upon an ontological and epistemological distinction made between 'the Orient' and 'the Occident'" (*Said* 2). This binary opposite, which Said calls orientalism, is "best grasped as a set of constraints upon and limitation of thought [rather] than ... a positive doctrine" (42). As a diaspora Chinese scholar, Liang Qichao assumed an orientalist position and brought the gaze of the West into the buildup of a Chinese nation. His account of the development of human history betrays his way of thinking:

> Man in the lowest stage leads a nomadic life. Although he does not suffer from lack of food and clothes, he has no knowledge of machines. Although he possesses knowledge ofletters, he does not have learning. He always fears calamities and is dependent upon others' mercy and initiatives and waits for luck to come to him. Man in the semi-civilized stage engages in agriculture and builds cities and state. However, there are many flaws. There are few who engage in practical learning, though literature flourishes. Semicivilized man lacks creativity and inventiveness. Man in the enlightened stage is active and independent which enables him to get rid of old customs and to achieve self reliance. Not satisfied with a small ambition, he advances relentlessly to the future. In the enlightened stage knowledge is based upon practical learning as the foundation for creativity and invention. The development of commerce and industry is aimed at the happiness of the people (*zhuanji* v.8 9).

However, flawed his thinking was, Liang Qichao was eager to introduce nationalism to China and to form a unified China in idea and in practice. One strategy of Liang's nation-building efforts was to map what Chinese lacked in order to "grow newness." He was convinced by Fukuzawa Yukichi that the scientific spirit was among many things that the Chinese needed. The adventurous spirit expressed in *Deux ans de vacances* must be something Liang thought the Chinese also needed. In his essay "Xin min shuo" ("Discourse on the New Citizen"), he argues that "one of the reasons that Western nations are better than China is because they are full of adventurous spirit. This is the most important." That might explain in part why Liang translated that novel. Another reason could be that the children in the novel include an American, a French boy, and an aborigine from New Zealand as well as crowd of boys from England, all of whom have to cooperate with each other in order to survive. More importantly, out of his personal and reading experiences, Liang Qichao developed a particular understanding of the "new" which was deeply infected by utopian ideas. In 1902, in his novel *Xin Zhongguo wei lai ji* (The Future of a New China) and his essay "Xin min shuo" ("Discourse on the New Citizen"), Liang consistently expressed an idea that the Chinese people needed to renew their morality, language, and mind in order for the rebirth of China. To renew all of these, Chinese need to bring in foreign factors. In his book *Global Space and the Nationalist discourse of Modernity*, Xiaobing Tang traces the origin of Liang's idea of newness and points out that liberalism and nationalism are behind Liang's thinking: "The new that Liang [Qichao] was now able to explicate in *Discourse on the New Citizen*, therefore, is not merely a historical and philosophical necessity; it also implies an elite political agenda" (22).

Against this background, Liang Qichao translated Jules Verne's novel *Deux ans de vacances*. The first chapter of his translation appeared in *Xin Ming Cong Bao* (New People's Miscellany) in February 1902. Liang translated only the first 9 chapters; the remaining 9 chapters were translated by Luo Pu and serialized in the same newspaper. I will start with a comparison of the translations of passage in English, Japanese, and Chinese.

English translation:	Literal Chinese translation	Liang Qichao's translation

On the night of 9 March 1860, the clouds scudded so low they seemed to be lying on the ocean. The horizon had narrowed to a few yards. The 100-ton schooner Sloughie bounced about in a howling storm. Again and again she rose to mountainous waves in a waste of sea. The name painted on her stern could only be guessed. All that was left was an S and the ie. The crash of water, or a collision perhaps, had torn away part of the planking.

1860年3月9日夜，满天黑云低低地垂压在海面上。四周一片漆黑，难辨咫尺之外。这时，一只尚未扯其风帆的小船掠过巨浪，向着东方飞快地驶去。闪电不时划破天空照亮了小船的身影。

调寄摸鱼儿

莽重洋惊涛横雨，一叶破帆漂渡。入死出生人十五，都是髫龄乳稚。逢生处，更坠向天涯岛无归路，停辛伫苦。但抖擞精神，斩除荆棘，客我两年住。
英雄业，岂有天公能妒。殖民俨辟新土，赫赫国旗辉南极，好个共和制度。天不负，看马角乌头奏凯同归去。我非妄语。劝年少同胞听鸡起舞，休把此生误。

看官，你道这首词讲的是什么典故呢？ 话说距今四十二年前，正是西历一千八百六十年三月初九日。那晚上满天黑云，低飞压海，蒙蒙暗暗，咫尺不见。忽有一艘小船，好像飞一般，奔向东南去。

Liang's translation is much longer than the English and Japanese versions because he adds a poem that is not in the other two versions. As I have mentioned before, Chinese vernacular fiction often starts with a poem that indicates the moral or wisdom the author wants to express. To follow this convention, Liang composed a poem by himself and added it to his translation. This action suggests that Liang's Japanese is good enough that he has read the whole book and grasped the content and ideas of the original. The constraints placed by the vernacular fiction are also displayed in Liang's translation of the title and use of narrator. The original title of the first chapter is "Set off," while Liang translates it with a couplet which reads "A single ship in the vast earth; several children in the high sea." The invisible narrator in the original becomes a third person voice of the storyteller, which is a convention of the vernacular novel. The narration of the original goes in a flashback fashion. Liang Qichao is amazed by this technique and praises it as the strongest point of Western fiction. However, the plot in vernacular fiction unfolds in a straight line because the storyteller cannot narrate two lines of story at the same time. To accommodate the backlash narration in the original, Liang Qichao has to force the narrator to speak the story directly. In short, Liang Qichao's translation observes all the conventions of vernacular fiction regarding structure. Another conspicuous feature is that Liang Qichao does not practice a deletion strategy, a common strategy favored by other translators.

For different reasons, Lin Shu and Yan Fu decided to use classic Chinese in their translations. Though Liang Qichao translated in classical Chinese, he did change his language. In his "Translator's epilogue," Liang Qichao expected his translation "to be written all in vernacular Chinese, following the writing style of *Shui hu zhuan* (Water Margins) and *Hong lou meng* (Dream of the Red Chamber)." After years of advocating the use of ordinary people's language in writing, Liang's intention finally coincided with his political ideas. The result, however, was beyond his expectation, because

However, I felt this [using vernacular Chinese to translate] was very hard when I started to translate. It saved me a lot of work when I mixed it with classic Chinese. When I translated the first several chapters in vernacular Chinese, I could only finish 1,000 characters in an hour. This time I got 2,500 characters. I as the translator tried to save myself some time and had to use both vernacular and classic Chinese. I am aware of the inconsistency in style, but I will have to wait until the end of the translation for revision. This shows that the separation of written language and oral language is one of the worst disadvantages of Chinese literature. A literary revolution is no easy task.

When Liang Qichao claimed that he "translated the first several chapters in vernacular Chinese," he must have modeled his vernacular Chinese on the language of *San guo zhi yan yi (The Romance of the Three Kingdoms)*, a famous historical novel written by Luo Guanzhong (c. 1330-1400 BC). I am not going to dwell at the long history of the formation of fiction. Suffice it to say that the book was written in partly vernacular and partly classical Chinese. It is worth noting that with the development of the Chinese language, the vernacular language in *San guo zhi yan yi (The Romance of the Three Kingdoms)* was not a plain language to Liang Qichao's readers.

Moreover, Liang Qichao expressed a kind of dual attitude towards the use of language, an interesting phenomenon which distinguishes Liang's generation and the May-fourth Movement generation in terms of using vernacular Chinese. Zhou Zuoren (1885-1967), an extraordinary Chinese writer and translator and brother of Lu Xun, makes a cogent comment on the difference in question:

Nowadays, our writing attitude is unified, that is: no matter who the audience is, no matter what we do, no matter whether we compose a book or write a message note, we invariably use *bai hua* [plain language]. The writing attitude was dual in the past: not all writings were written in bai hua. Only ill-educated ordinary people and workers wrote in *bai hua*...when it came to serious writings or books, classical Chinese was naturally used. Therefore, we come to the conclusion that in the past, classical Chinese used by and was used for "lords," while *bai hua* was by and for "servants" (56).

The fact that Liang Qichao wrote much faster in classical Chinese than in vernacular Chinese suggests that Liang felt more comfortable with classical Chinese, which functioned as mother tongue for him. However, the power of the (political) novel lies solely in its popularity among ordinary people who speak vernacular language. His political commitment to enlightenment not only reminds him of the "inconsistency in style," but also raises a question for him about how to bridge the linguistic and ideological gap between himself and his target audience. Liang Qichao came up with the solution of using "both vernacular and classic Chinese." This solution was not satisfactory in part because the vernacular Chinese he used in this translation was neither his nor his readers' language. The most important reason was the Chinese language was diversified, so were the people and the nation into which he translated, a fact that rendered a perfect solution impossible.

Liang Qichao's translation of *Deux ans de vacances* was supported by his political aim of introducing nationalism and building a new Chinese nation. Scholars have long argued that fiction is one of main sites of the formation of national consciousness. In his important anthology *Nation and Narration*, Homi K. Bhabha investigates the function of fiction to interpellate and concludes that "the scrapes, patches, and rags of daily life must be repeatedly turned into the signs of a national culture, while the very act of the narrative performance interpellates a growing circle of national subjects" (297). While Liang's translation of fiction intended to interpellate subjects for China, the daily life of the Chinese people could not be turned into a national culture. On the contrary, what Liang Qichao did was to hybridize Chinese culture by mixing classic Chinese, vernacular Chinese, Japanese neologisms, and Western concepts. According to Liang, China was in transition and a new China is in the future. Translation served as the bridge to the future.

Chapter Four

CONCLUSION

In the previous chapters, I have discussed the different roles of historical, ideological, and literary factors that conditioned the translation strategies of Lin Shu, Yan Fu, and Liang Qichao. Motivated by his proclaimed intention "to cultivate patriotism and preserve the [Chinese] race" (*Yan* 206), Lin Shu started translating Harriet Beecher Stowe's *Uncle Tom's Cabin* in response partly to the anti-Chinese law, the *Exclusion Act of California*, in America and partly to the high patriotic sentiment in China. In the long history of team translation in China, the working relationship between Lin Shu and his collaborator Wei Yi was an exception, because Lin Shu, who had no knowledge of the source language, dominated the translating process and earned his reputation as an expert translator by rewriting an oral rendition of the source text. Lin Shu's mastery of classic Chinese contributed to his hegemony over his collaborator while his sinicizing interpretations of foreign themes, genres, and literary techniques led to the popular acceptance of his translation. The private publishing industry whose success was dependent on profits sponsored

Lin Shu's translation. As a result, marketability not only influenced Lin Shu's translation techniques such as omission, deletion, and paraphrase, but also competed with ideology in realizing Lin Shu's political agenda.

With the similar political intention to transform China into a powerful and wealthy country, Yan Fu translated Thomas Henry Huxley's *Evolution and Ethics* after the failure of the government-led modernization efforts, marked by the thwarted Hundred Days' Reform. With a highly stylistic classic Chinese, Yan Fu introduced to Chinese literati a progressive historical thinking and a world picture in which China had to "struggle for existence." Targeting an elite Chinese literati who wielded political and ideological power, Yan Fu displayed a tendency to overtranslate by making his translation of Huxley read more like a pre-Qin essay, an approach sanctioned by an "undifferentiated" sponsor Wu Rulun. Equally, he tried to justify his three principles for a good translation by citing Confucian and Buddhist canons, a move to assure the acceptance of his translation by his target audience. Though his attempt at acceptance and popularity was not at the price of loyalty to the original, he tried to foreground the original arguments that were conducive to the formation of the Chinese identity by restructuring, Sinicizing, and overtranslating the source text.

A representative of the so-called "heroic translation," a free translation strategy popular in the late Qing era, Liang Qichao was known for his audacity and violence when it came to deal with the source text. Besides his language inefficiency, his incorrigible political impetus always overpowered his aesthetic considerations and guided him to rewrite the original in order to serve his political purpose. His promotion of the genre of the political fiction didn't achieve his goal to elevate the status of fiction in the Chinese literary system, but his ideas of newness, modern China, and literature's political function had a great impact on both Chinese literati and the general public. His translation of Jules Verne's 1888 novel *Deux ans de vacances* was based on the Japanese translation by Morita Shiken, who translated from the English version of the French text. The adventurous spirit expressed in the original was emphasized and incorporated into his project of the redefinition of China during his exile years in Japan. More importantly, he borrowed many Japanese *kanjis* and expressions in his translation and started to establish his famous writing style. This "new style" with its massive use of colloquial expressions, neologisms, and foreign terms violently transformed the traditional Chinese writing style. In sum, notwithstanding their different opinions on translation, the three translators not only introduced ideas of anti-slavery, evolution, and adventure, but also transformed the Chinese people's traditional worldview. Under Western eyes, the comfortable image of China as the center of the world dissolved and the concept of China as "an imagined political community—and imagined as both inherently limited and sovereign" (*Anderson*, 1991: 6) began to emerge. Moreover, both Yan Fu and Lin Shu's depressing picture of China and Liang Qichao's expectation in the future expressed a strong sense of emergency that was indispensable to the formation of Chinese identity.

Translation, Patronage, and Power

The years during which these three translators developed their skills witnessed the decline of Chinese political and literary dominance and a fast transition through various paradigms under Western influences. Scholars have noted that the closeness between real politics and literary presentations contributed both to the popularity of their translations at the time and their rapid descent into oblivion since their day. The fall into oblivion of their translations was acclaimed by critics such as Qu Qiubai. In a series of letters discussing translation with Lu Xun, Qu Qiubai (1899-1935), a famous communist leader and translator, acknowledged only the historical value of Lin Shu, Yan Fu, and Liang Qichao. According to Qu, the only reason later generations of readers would read them was to ridicule their efforts to stick with classic conventions against the grain. He denied any initiatives shown by those three authors to renew Chinese language and literature. Therefore, he called for putting the works of the three authors in the historical museum of China (*Luo* 287). Qu's argument suggests that translations of the three translators immediately lost their aesthetic appeal to the reader once Western political ideas expressed in translations were replaced by more radical or revolutionary ideas. On the contrary, in his study on alternative modernities embedded in late Qing fiction, David Der-wei Wang argues that late Qing translations introduced foreign models for Chinese literati and deserve serious study for their impact on the development of literature. He points out that late Qing translations contain complex aesthetic factors and "late Qing translators used translations to serve emotive and ideological goals inconceivable to the original authors and that these translators' witting and unwitting misinterpretations of the originals generated spontaneous alternative versions of the modern" (*Wang* 3). Despite the difference between their evaluations, the two scholars share the same assumption that translation is merely a means to convey the meaning of the original. I argue that this idea of translation oversimplifies the relationship among translation, translator and politics and fails to understand the complex tensions between aesthetic considerations and political commitments in translation.

My study has shown that Andre Lefevere's concept of patronage is a very useful tool in analyzing the relationship between translation and politics. According to Lefevere, patronage has as many forms as person(s), a religious body, a political party, a social class, a court, and publishers. Different from critics and editors, who are mainly concerned about the poetics of translation, patronage is usually "more interested in the ideology" of translation (*Lefevere* 17). By studying the nature of patronage of a translator, we will understand how politics exerts its power on the translation.

Though all three Chinese translators published their translations through private publishers, there remained a huge difference in the nature of the relationship between them and their patronage. Among the three translators, Yan Fu cared least about the marketability of his translations. I have described the situation of the publication of his *Tian yan lun*. It demonstrates that the profit motive never occurred to Yan Fu when he translated. It was Wu Rulun who functioned as his patron in that Wu endorsed Yan Fu's new ideas and certified Yan Fu's status as master essayist. Liang Qichao was a professional politician and usually published his translations in the newspapers he edited. Financially supported by donors and his friends, his newspapers had less financial burden and depended less on market forces. Liang Qichao used his newspapers as the organ to promote his political ideas and to educate the masses. The reason he used plain language in his writings and translations was to make his ideas available to every Chinese. Lin Shu was a professional translator and had to consider seriously his readership whose characteristics have been shaped by traditional cultures and ideologies. In his translator's prefaces, he often bridged the cultural and moral gaps between his readers and the books he translated. This consideration led him to draw a startling analogy between the courtesan Marguerite and two distinguished Chinese ministers, aiming at justifying his translation of Dumas *fils*'s fiction and attracting readers. He appreciated this sentimental romance because "the way Marguerite served Armand is the same way Long and Bi served their emperors Jie and Zhou. As Long and Bi had no regrets even though the emperors killed them, Marguerite had none when Armand 'killed' her. Thus, I say, in this world, only the like of Long and Bi could compare with Marguerite" (*Bali cha hua nü yi shi* 1). Here Lin deploys the domesticating strategy for an acceptable translation.

The controversies around his translation of Rider Haggard's *John Haste* provide us with a good opportunity to understand clearly the historical, cultural, and political situation surrounding Lin Shu's strategy of translation. *John Haste* was first translated into Chinese by Yang Zilin and published by the Wen Ming (Civilization) Press in 1901. In the translator's preface, Yang said he found this book in a used bookstore. The first part of the book was missing, and he chose to translate the second part in that the heroine desired to give her lover happiness at the price of her own love and life, a feminine ideal that was consistent with Confucian ethics. In view of the great popularity and high quality of the book, Lin Shu had the complete translation published by the Commercial Press in 1905. Surprisingly Lin's complete version provoked criticism because the passages purposely omitted from Yang's version dealt with the pregnancy of an unmarried girl and her marriage without the permission of her parents, something that was obviously against traditional ethical codes. Songchen's opinion was representative. For the sake of China society, he favored Yang's selective choice and worried that the translation might bring wrong ideas into China. He warned translators "no later than several decades from now, the customs of shaking hands and kissing might spread all over the China" (172).

However, despite being a reformer and, later, a conservative who claimed himself to be a guardian of classical civilization, Lin was aware of the violent power of Western fiction and intended to place translation in the self-strengthening agenda whose primary goal was to save the decayed Qing imperial dynasty with the help of Western science and technology. Guided by this intention, patriotism was chosen by Lin as an ideological strategy to balance the translator's political agenda and the readership's conventions. In his preface to *Ai guo er tong zi zhuan* (Stories of Two Patriotic Boys), Lin Shu expressed his thoughts that "today's China is feckless and declining. It's a great pity that I do not have wide knowledge, so that I could come up with original works for publication to inspire my countrymen. What I can do is to translate as many as I can of the stories of Western heroes in order that my people can, by learning from these heroes, get out of their state of lassitude and isolation, and catch up with the strong rival nations" (3). In the name of patriotism Lin had an opportunity to introduce Western thought without offending his readers.

The different strategies applied to with the translation of religious passages in the originals by Lin demonstrate how patriotism functioned regarding Lin's translations. Tightly linked with the military, economical, and cultural invasion of imperialists, missionaries aroused strong anti-foreigner sentiment and Christianity became a sensitive issue at all levels. In his translation of Daniel Defoe's *Robinson Crusoe*, Lin Shu retained all passages regarding Christianity using the excuse of loyalty to the originals. However, when he left the same kind of parts untranslated in his rendition of Harriet B. Stowe's *Uncle Tom's Cabin*, Lin's excuse was "for the reader's sake." In fact, the reason for Lin to translate *Robinson Crusoe* was to promote Crusoe's sense of adventure, his unyielding spirit in moments of adversity, and his resourcefulness when confronting nature, compared to the lethargic and pusillanimous lives most Chinese people lived. The introduction of Christian ideas that helped Crusoe live through the crisis might be useful for Chinese. Lin translated *Uncle Tom's Cabin* in 1901, a time when the *Exclusion Act of California* was in force. In his review of this book, Lin commented, "the calamity is about to befall upon our yellow race: the exclusion of Chinese laborers in the U.S. and the maltreatment of Chinese in various countries in the West are already a fact. Their predicament was in no way different from that of the Negroes, but worse than the latter" (*Hei nu xu tian lu* 1). Therefore, his strategy to omit certain passages both fulfilled his political task and satisfied his readers' taste.

In short, politics set ideological constraints for the translations of Yan Fu, Lin Shu and Liang Qichao and exerted great power on their selections of original texts, translation strategies, and publication and reception of their translations. However, this does not mean that their translations were only a tool to serve their political and social ends. In fact, these translators took poetics seriously when translating and their translations introduced into China new aesthetic forms and tastes, which laid a foundation for modern Chinese literature. The most important contribution of their translations, I argue, was the keen awareness of language and the efforts at creating a new Chinese language in an era of political and social turmoils. A new sense of Chineseness grew among their readers when their translations rendered China and the West in an unequal relationship. This kind of thinking of a new language for the Chinese people is the place where the political consideration of these translators met their poetic consideration.

Translation, Mother Tongue, and Poetics

Exemplified in the works of Gayatri Chakravorty Spivak and Tejaswini Niranjana, postcolonial translation studies focuses attention on analyzing power relations that function in colonial translation projects and aims at deconstructing Western hegemonic representations of the Orient. In her seminal paper "The Politics of Translation," Spivak takes issue with the language used in English translations of Third World literature by exploring power, desire, and historicity of language. Against the literal or figurative usage of language in English translations, she tries to engage language with historical and social moment when the gendered subjectivity of the speaker surfaces. According to her, "language isn't everything. It is only a vital clue to where the self loses its boundaries." Based on her experiences in translating Bengali literature into English, she draws the conclusion that because English is a hegemonic language of the colonizers, English translations often assimilate Bengali experiences and fail to express the difference between the two literatures. She argues, "In the act of wholesale translation into English there can be a betrayal of the democratic ideal into the law of the strongest. This happens when all the literature of the Third world gets translated into a sort of with-it translatese, so that the literature by a woman in Palestine begins to resemble, in the feel of its prose, something by a man in Taiwan" (*Spivak* 182). Spivak concedes that full communication between the original and its readers can never be achieved, because translation is never complete and always in process. But she leaves the translator a difficult political task, namely, to bring the English-speaking reader as close as possible to the authentic experience of Third World people. By linking translation to the colonial discourse of Orientalism, Tejaswini Niranjana calls into question the myth of translation as "a transparent presentation of something that already exists," a powerful strategy used by Western colonizers in "fixing" colonized cultures (3). Rather, she attempts to explore "the asymmetry and inequality of relations between peoples, races, languages" (1) and tends to view translation as a form of resistance to colonial subjugation. Though she is critiqued for her mistreatment of the great Indian translator A. K. Ramanujan, Niranjana's reading of English translations of Southern Indian poems demonstrates that the colonial power attempted to assimilate Indian poetry to the discourses of Christianity. By counterattacking this assimilative strategy, she advocates an "interventionist" approach to resist the containment of colonial discourse and foregrounds the foreignness of the original Indian factors in translation. Behind her translation strategy lies her great political ambition to put together the fragmentary history and memory of the colonized. Postcolonial translation studies powerfully demonstrate the close connection between colonization and translation: translation played an important role in the colonial administrative, educational, and ideological systems and helped to internalize fixed and distorted images of the colonized; colonial powers sponsored numerous translation projects that aimed to translate indigenous literatures into hegemonic languages, especially English, and supported the dominance of Western cultural imperialism.

Postcolonial translation studies open a door for students of late Qing translations when it comes to answer questions such as how politics has influenced Chinese translators' choices of translation strategies. How was translation used as a tool of resistance in struggles against Western colonizers? How did Chinese translators maintain the status of the Chinese language in the face of the introduction of foreign languages? However, many conclusions of postcolonial translation studies cannot be applicable to China because of several major differences between China and India, the country from which Spivak and Niranjana both have drawn their conclusions. Firstly, the translations discussed in postcolonial translation studies are from indigenous languages to English, while late Qing translations in question are Chinese translations of Western works. The direction of the flow of languages matters because the status of the source language has great impact on a translator's choice of translation strategy. In English translations of Indian literature, misrepresentations of the colonized can be argued for anticolonial causes, while the misrepresentation of Western culture and authors in a late Qing translation took on a different political color. Secondly, literary tradition exerts more impact on Chinese writers and translators than on their Indian counterparts. As Niranjana has shown, Indian translators tended to conform to the discourses of Western traditions in order to gain the acceptance of their translation of Saivite poetry in British. On the contrary, Lin Shu and Liang Qichao's handling of the original stories was visibly influenced by the Chinese story-telling tradition while Yan Fu intentionally indulged himself in the pre-Qin literary and writing style. I have shown in my discussion that norms of traditional Chinese literature governed the three Chinese translators' translations. Thirdly, late Qing Chinese translators had a different perception of Western culture and science from that of postcolonial scholars. Despite the strong patriotic sentiment against imperialism harbored in Lin Shu, Yan Fu, and Liang Qichao, they all recognized that Western technology, science, and political systems outranked those of China. As a result, when they translated foreign works, they attempted to introduce new ideas and knowledge into China. The postcolonial theme of challenging Western distorted images of the colonized never occurred to them.

Those differences suggest that late Qing translation of Western works cannot fall exactly in the model proposed by postcolonial translation scholars, even if late Qing translation also carried the load of identity-building and nation-building. Spivak believes that in translation one could "get around the confines of one's 'identity'," because translation provides a chance to experience the "contained alterity in an unknown language spoken in a different cultural milieu" (181). However, in translation late Qing translators dealt with a different problematic and intended to seek for affinity between the alterity "in an unknown language" and the familiar language, expressed perfectly by Yan Fu's *xin-da-ya* principle. In Lin Shu's classic Chinese contaminated by colloquial Chinese, in Yan Fu's beautiful pre-Qin style classic Chinese, in Liang Qichao's new journalistic Chinese influenced by Japanese, the problematic of mother tongue emerged on the scene at the end of the nineteenth century.

To late Qing translators, the problematic of the mother tongue was posed first as a historical question. Officially, the Qing dynasty was a bilingual state in that Manchu was an official language along with Chinese. With the assimilation of Manchu culture into Han Chinese culture for political reasons, Chinese soon regained its predominant status in political and administrative circumstances and continued its monopoly in literature. Manchu exerted no influence on literature and Chinese literati were never required or intended to learn this "official language." In a sense, China was a unilingual country in the Qing Dynasty with Chinese as the only language. No matter one's ethnicity, one had to compose in Chinese to be called a man of letters.* There were two forms of Chinese: one was classic Chinese, the other vernacular Chinese. It is well known that classic Chinese was a language used only by literati in composing poetry, prose, and, sometimes, fiction. In addition, it was the language used in official documents and

---

* The most prominent Manchu writer of *ci*, a kind of poetry, was Nalan Xingde (1655-1685) who was known for his mastery of Chinese.

functioned as a standard language. Vernacular Chinese was mainly a spoken language, but vernacular fiction gradually gained acceptance as a literary genre after the creation of *The Romance of the Three Kingdoms*. Since the 1840s, the private publishing industry was on the rise and newspapers facilitated the spread of vernacular Chinese. Though the concerted call for standardizing Chinese with vernacular language had to wait another decade, Lin Shu, Yan Fu, and Liang Qichao were facing difficulty in choosing a language for translation, an act to make sense of themselves politically and culturally. Lin Shu and Yan Fu chose classical Chinese and identified with traditional Chinese culture while Liang Qichao was inclined towards vernacular Chinese and embraced radical political thought. Their different choices are very interesting if one takes into consideration their educational background. Lin Shu and Yan Fu received little school education in classics and had a problem in receiving degrees in the Imperial Examinations.* Surprisingly, both of them ended up translating in classic Chinese, a hegemonic language other than the language they grew up with. According to Qian Zhongshu, Lin Shu's classic Chinese contains many vernacular expressions and allows more grammatical freedom than in typical classic essays (1108). The fact that Yan Fu's translation received high praise from the classic master Wu Rulun demonstrates Yan Fu's wonderful skill in classic Chinese. My juxtaposition of Huxley's original and Yan Fu's translation showed that Yan Fu abided by his pre-Qin expression principle partly by citing directly from pre-Qin classics. Acclaimed as the "genius of Guangdong," Liang Qichao got his *ju ren* degree (quasi-master) at the age of 16. He studied Confucian classics under the guidance of Kang Youwei, one of the

---

* Lin Shu got his *xiu cai* degree (quasi-bachelor) in 1882 when he was 30 years old, but failed to get any higher degree despite several attempts. Yan Fu failed six times in the lowest level Imperial Examinations and earned no degree.

most famous late Qing scholars. Rather than living comfortably in classic Chinese, Liang became one of the first newsmen and translators who used vernacular Chinese in serious writing. His vernacular Chinese was characterized by a mixture of Japanese loanwords, classic Chinese expressions, and journalistic style. His writing style remained unchanged even after the New Cultural Movement in 1915 which introduced a standardized vernacular Chinese.

The stories of the three Chinese translators choosing the language they were unfamiliar with seem to prove Spivak's point that speaking in a language that is not one's own language is a way of mind-changing and double-writing, a necessary step for translators to register the "history of the language, the history of the author's moment, the history of the language-in-translation" (*Spivak* 186). In fact, the three Chinese translators did not attempt to explore the alterity in another language whose specific historical situation was indispensable to the understanding of the formation of the colonial subjectivity. Rather, they aimed at an affinity among languages that would lead to a new language that they had not acquired. In translation, they not only tested the plasticity of the Chinese language in accommodating foreign languages, but also destabilized the boundary within the Chinese language. By using an unfamiliar language to translate an unknown language, the three Chinese translators longed for a new Chinese language that would become the mother tongue of the Chinese people as opposed to other races and ethnicities. But the imperfectness of their language suggested that late Qing translators were in a state of aphasia. Working among classic Chinese, vernacular Chinese, and a foreign language, different translators had to lean towards one language in their effort to achieve the affinity. They all exhibited symptoms of aphasia: Lin Shu's poor enunciation when he mixed his classic Chinese with colloquial expressions; Yan

Fu's inability to write/speak when he struggled to find exact translations for foreign terms; Liang Qichao's excessive use of personal neologisms when he borrowed Japanese words that were hard to understand to his Chinese readers.

In reality, their efforts to overcome aphasia paid off when a standardized Chinese came into being some years later as a result of the critical reactions to the three translators. Moreover, out of the pursuit of affinity by late Qing translators, Chinese translators of later generations favored the translation strategy of assimilating foreign factors into the standardized Chinese, or in other words, the politically dominant language at a given historical moment. Sun Ge argues that the assimilation strategy results in the loss of the "bilingualness" inherent in any translation and the construction of a Chinese tradition on the basis of dominant ideology (*Sun* xxiv-xxxi). As a "monstrosity" of translation, Lu Xun's staunch literal translation strategy echoes Walter Benjamin's idea of translation as the expression of "the central reciprocal relationship between languages" (*Benjamin* 72). Lun Xu's introduction of literatures of weak nations by his "hard translation" expresses his foregrounding of alterity and uncompromising gesture toward Western imperialism and domestic powers (See *Cheung*, 2001).

Despite the assimilating strategy used by Lin Shu, Yan Fu, and Liang Qichao, their translation effort resonates strangely with Benjamin's idea of translation as the afterlife of the original. In his provocative paper "The Task of the Translator," Benjamin makes a connection between translation and afterlife: "For a translation comes later than the original, and since the important works of world literature never find their chosen translators at the time of their origin, their translation marks their stage of continued life. The idea of life and afterlife in works of art should be regarded with an entirely unmetaphorical objectivity"

(71). Translation, therefore, assures the original a "potentially eternal afterlife in succeeding generations." The three Chinese translators made their own effort to give Chinese an "eternal afterlife."

Bibliography

Ahmad, Aijaz. "Jameson's Rhetoric of Otherness and the 'National Allegory'." *Social Text* 17 (1987): 3-25.

A Ying 阿英. *Wan Qing xi qu xiao shuo mu lu* 晚清戏曲小说目录 *[A Bibliographical Survey of Drama and Fiction in the Late Qing Dynasty]*. Shanghai: Shanghai gu dian wen xue chu ban she, 1957.
_____. *Wan Qing xiao shuo shi* 晚清小说史 *[History of Late Qing Dynasty Fiction]*. Beijing: Zuo jia chu ban she, 1955.

Ban, Gu 班固. *Han shu* 漢書 *[Historical Records of Han Dynasty]*. Shanghai: Shanghai gu ji chu ban she, 1986.

Benjamin, Walter. *Illuminations*. Trans. Harry Zohn. New York: Schocken Press, 1969.

Bhabha, Homi K. *Nation and Narration*. London and New York: Routledge, 1990.

Chang, Hao. *Liang Ch'i-ch'ao and Intellectual Transition in China, 1890-1907*. Cambridge: Harvard University Press, 1971.

Chatterjee, Partha. *Nationalist Thought and the Colonial World*. London: Zed Books for the United Nations University, 1986.

Chen, Pingyuan 陈平原 and Xia, Xiaohong 夏晓红, ed. *Er shi shi ji Zhongguo xiao shuo li lun zi liao* 二十世纪中国小说理论资料 *[Theoretical Materials on Chinese Novel in the Twentieth Century]*. Beijing: Beijing da xue chu ban she, 1989.

Chen, Zhaoying 陳昭瑛. "Lun Taiwan ben tu hua yun dong: yi ge wen hua shi de kao cha 論台灣本土化運動：一個文化史的考察 The Localization Movement in Taiwan: A Cultural Historical Investigation." *Zhong wai wen xue* 中外文學 *(Chinese and Foreign literatures)* 23.9 (1995): 142-47.

Cheung, Lik Kwan 張歷君. "Towards the Pure Language: Re-Interpreting Walter Benjamin's Translation Theory through Lu Xun's Practice of "Hard Translation"." *Zhong wai wen xue* 中外文學 *(Chinese and Foreign literatures)* 30.7 (2001): 128-58.

Cheung, Martha P. Y. "The Discourse of Occidentalism? Wei Yi and Lin Shu's Treatment of Religious Material in Their Translation of *Uncle Tom's Cabin.*" In *Translation and Creation: Readings of Western Literature in Early Modern China, 1840-1918.* Ed. David Pollard. Amsterdam: John Benjamins, 1998.

Ching, Leo T. S. *Becoming "Japanese": Colonial Taiwan and the Politics of Identity Formation.* Berkeley and Los Angeles: University of California Press. 2001

Compton, Robert W. *A Study of the Translations of Lin Shu, 1852-1934.* Ph.D. Diss. Stanford University, 1971.

Eoyang, Eugene Chen. *The Transparent Eye: Reflections on Translation, Chinese Literature, and Comparative Poetics.* Honolulu: University of Hawaii Press, 1993.

Evan-Zohar, Itamar. "Papers in Historical Poetics." *Papers on Poetics and Semiotics 8.* Ed. Benjamin Hrushovski and Itamar Even-Zohar. Tel Aviv: University Publishing Projects, 1978.
_____. "Polysystem Theory." *Poetics* Today 1:2 (1979): 237-310.
_____. "Translation Theory Today: A Call for Transfer Theory." *Poetics Today* 2:4 (1981): 1-7.

Ding, Wenjiang 丁文江, ed. Liang Qichao nian pu chang bian chu gao 梁啟超年譜長編初稿 [First Draft of the Timeline of Liang Qichao's Life]. Taibei: Zhong hua shu ju, 1959.

Feldman, Horace Z. "The Meiji Political Novel: A Brief Survey." *The Far Eastern Quarterly* 9.3 (1950): 245-55.

Feng, Ziyou 冯自由. *Ge ming yi shi* 革命逸史 *[An Anecdotal History of Revolution]*. Vol. 3. 5 vols. Taibei: Shang wu yin shu guan, 1965.

Gentzler, Edwin. *Contemporary Translation Theories*. London and New York: Routledge, 1992.

Gries, Peter Hays. *China's New Nationalism: Pride, Politics, and Diplomacy*. Berkeley: University of California Press, 2004.

Guo, Yanli 郭延礼. *Zhongguo jin dai fan yi wen xue gai lun* 中国近代翻译文学概论 *[Translated Literature of Modern China: An Introduction]*. Wuhan: Hubei jiao yu chu ban she, 1998.

Hanan, Patrick. *Chinese Fiction of the Nineteenth and Early Twentieth Centuries*. NY: Columbia University Press, 2004.
————. *The Chinese Vernacular Story*. Cambridge: Harvard University Press, 1981.

Hanguang, 寒光. *Lin Qinnan* 林琴南. Shanghai: Zhong hua shu ju, 1935.
Harvie, Christopher T. *Centre of Things: Political Fiction in Britain from Disraeli to the Present*. London: Unwin Hyman, 1991.

Hermans, Theo. "Cross-Cultural Translation Studies as Thick Translation." *Bulletin of the School of Oriental & African Studies* 66 (2003): 380-89.
————, ed. *Crosscultural Transgressions : Research Models in Translation Studies I: Historical and Ideological Issues*. Manchester, UK and Northampton, MA: St. Jerome Publishing, 2002.
Hsia, C.T. *The classic Chinese Novel: A Critical Introduction*. Bloomington: Indiana University Press, 1968.
————. *A History of Modern Chinese Fiction*. New Haven: Yale University Press, 1961.
————. "Yen Fu and Liang Ch'i-Ch'ao as Advocates of New Fiction." *Chinese Approaches to Literature from Confucius to Liang Ch'i-Ch'ao*. Ed. Adele Richett. New Heaven: Princeton University Press, 1978.

Hu, Shi 胡適. *Si shi zi shu* 四十自述 *[Autobiography]*. Shanghai: Ya dong tu shu guan, 1939.

Hu, Ying. *Tales of Translation: Composing the New Women in China, 1899-1918*. Stanford: Starnford UP, 2000.

Huang, Jun 黄濬. *Huasuiren sheng an zhi yi* 花隨人聖盦摭憶 *[Recollections from Huasuiren Cloister]*. Shanghai: Shanghai gu ji shu dian, 1983.

Huang, Ko-wu. In *Search of Power, Wealth, and Freedom: Yan Fu and the Origins of Modern Chinese Liberalism*. Diss. Stanford University, 2001.

Huang, Philip. *Liang Ch'i-ch'ao and Modern Chinese Liberalism*. Seattle: University of Washington Press, 1972.

Huters, Theodore. "A New Way of Writing: The Possibilities for Literature in Late Qing China, 1895-1908." *Modern China* 14.3 (1988): 243-76.

Huxley, Thomas Henry. *Evolution and Ethics, and Other Essays*. New York: D. Appleton and company, 1911.
Jameson, Fredric. *The Jameson Reader*. Ed. Hardt, Michael and Kathi Weeks. Oxford: Blackwell, 2000.

Jiang, Shuzhuo 蒋述卓. *Fo jing chuan yi yu zhong gu wen xue si chao* 佛经传译与中古文学思潮 *[Translations of Buddhism and the Trends of Medieval Literature]*. Nanjing: Jiangxi wen yi, 1990.

Kang, Youwei 康有為. "Qinnan xian sheng xie wanmucaotang tu ti shi jian zeng fu xie 琴南先生寫萬木草堂圖題詩見贈賦謝 (A Poem to Thank Mr. Qinnan's Wanmucaotang Painting and Poem)." *Yong yan* 庸言 1.7 (1913): 1.

Keene, Donald. *Dawn to the West: Japanese Literature of the Modern Era, Fiction*. New York: Holt, Rinehart & Winston, 1984.

Lee, Leo Ou-fan. *Land Without Ghosts: Chinese Impressions of America From the Mid-nineteenth Century to the Present*. Berkeley: London University of California Press, 1989.
_____. "Lin Shu and His Translations: Western Fiction in Chinese Perspective." Papers on China 19 (1965):159.

Lefevere, Andre. *Translation, Rewriting, and the Manipulation of Literary Fame.* London and New York: Routledge, 1992.

Levenson, Joseph Richmond. *Liang Ch'i-ch'ao and the Mind of Modern China.* Cambridge: Harvard University Press, 1953.

Liang, Qichao 梁啓超. *Yin bing shi he ji [Collected Writings from the Ice-Drinkers Studio].* 12 vols. Beijing: Zhonghua shu ju, 1989.

Liao, Zhaoyang 廖朝陽. "Zhongguo ren de bei qing: hui ying Chen Zhaoying bing lun wen hua jian gou he min zu ren tong 中國人的悲情：回應陳昭瑛並論文化建構何民族認同 The Tragic Mentality of the Chinese People: A Response to Chen Zhaoying and My View of Cultural Construction and National Identity." *Zhong wai wen xue* 中外文學 *(Chinese and Foreign literatures)* 23.10 (1995): 102-26.

Lin, Shu 林纾. *Ai guo er tong zi zhuan* 愛國二童子傳 *(Stories of Two Patriotic Boys).* Shanghai: Shang wu yin shu guan, 1914.
_____. *Bali cha hua nü yi shi* 巴黎茶花女遺事. Beijing: Shang wu yin shu guan, 1981.
_____. *Hei nu xu tian lu* 黑奴吁天录 *(Black Slaves Sigh to the Heaven).* Beijing: Shang wu yin shu guan, 1981.
_____. *Xiao nü nai'er zhuan* 孝女耐兒傳 *(The Story of a Filial Daughter).* Shanghai: Shang wu yin shu guan, 1914.
_____. *Xiliya jun zhu bie zhuan* 西利亚郡主别传 *(Biography of Princess Cecilia).* Shanghai: Shang wu yin shu guan, 1914.

Liu, Lydia. *Translingual Practice: Literature, National Culture, and Translated Modernity—China, 1900-1937.* Stanford: Stanford University Press, 1995.
Luo, Xinzhang 羅新璋, ed. *Fan yi lun ji* 翻譯論集 *[Essays on Translation].* Beijing: Shang wu yin shu guan, 1984.
Lu, Xun 鲁迅. "Guan yu fan yi de tong xin 关于翻译的通信 [Correspondences on Translation]." *Lu Xun quan ji* 鲁迅全集 *[Completed Works of Lu Xun].* Vol. 4. Beijing: Ren min wen xue chu ban she, 1981. 370-88.
_____. "Zhongguo xiao shuo shi lue 中国小说史略 [A Concise History of Chinese Fiction]." *Lu Xun Quan Ji* 鲁迅全集 *[Complete Works of Lu Xun].* Vol. 9. Beijing: Ren ming wen xue chu ban she, 1981. 1-300.

Ma, Zuyi 马祖毅. *Zhongguo fan yi jian shi: "Wu si" yi qian bu fen* 中国 翻译简史：五四以前部分 *[A Brief History of Translation in China: Before the May Fourth Movement]*. Beijing: Zhongguo dui wai fan yi chu ban gong si, 1984.

Masini, Federico. The Formation of Modern Chinese Lexicon and its Evolution Toward a National Language: the Period from 1840-1898. In: *Journal of Chinese Linguistics, Monograph Series* 6 (1993).

Meng, Yuanlao 孟元老. *Dongjing meng hua lu* 東京夢華錄 *[Records of the Dreamlike Prosperity of the Eastern Capital]*. Shanghai: Gu dian wen xue chu ban she, 1956.

Moichi, Yoriko. "Japanese Utopian Literature from the 1870s to the Present and the Influence of Western Utopianism." *Utopian Studies* 10.2 (1999): 89.

Mori, Tokihiko. "Liang Qichao and Western Modernity: An Analysis of His Translations of the Term "Political Economy"." *The Role of Japan in Liang Qichao's Introduction of Modern Western Civilization to China*. Ed. Joshua A. Fogel. Berkeley: Center for Chinese Studies, Institute of East Asian Studies, University of California, 2004. 15-39.

Munday, Jeremy. *Introducing Translation Studies: Theories and Applications*. London and New York: Routledge, 2001.
Niranjana, Tejaswini. *Siting Translation: History, Post-structuralism, and the Colonial Context*. Berkeley: University of California Press, 1992.

Owen, Stephen, ed. *Readings in Chinese Literary Thought*. Combridge, Mass: Harvard University Press, 1992.

Qian, Jibo 錢基博. *Xian dai Zhongguo wen xue shi* 現代中國文學史 *[History of Modern Chinese Literature]*. Shanghai: Shi jie shu ju, 1933.
Qian, Xuantong 钱玄同. "Ji Chen Duxiu 寄陈独秀 (To Chen Duxiu)." *Xin qing nian* 新青年 *(New Youth)* 3.1 (1917):3.

Qian, Zhongshu. *Qian Zhongshu ji* 钱钟书集 *[Collected Works of Qian Zhongshu]*. Beijing: Sheng huo du shu xin zhi san lian shu dian, 2001.
Rolston, David L. *Traditional Chinese Fiction and Fiction Commentary: Reading and Writing Between the Lines*. Stanford: Stanford University Press, 1997.

Ruan, Yuan 阮元, ed. *Shi san jing zhu shu* 十三經注疏 *[Notes & Annotations to the 13 Classics]*. 1879. 2 vols. Beijing: Zhonghua shu ju, 1980.

Said, Edward. *Orientalism*. Toronto: Random House, 1994.

Sakaki, Atsuko. "Kajin No Kigu: The Meiji Political Novel and the Boundaries of Literature." *Monumenta Nipponica* 55.1 (2000): 83-108.
Schwartz, Benjamin. *In Search of Wealth and Power: Yen Fu and West*. Cambridge: Harvard UP, 1964.

Shen, Suru 沈苏儒. *Lun xin da ya: Yan Fu fan yi li lun yan jiu* 论信达雅：严复翻译理论研究 *[On Fidelity, Comprehensibility, and Elegance: Yan Fu's Translation Theory]*. Beijing: Shang wu yin shu guan, 1998.

Shi, Zanning 釋贊寧. *Song gao seng zhuan* 宋高僧傳 *[Biographies of Eminent Monks of Song Dynasty]*. 3 vols. Taibei: Wen shu chu ban she, 1988.

Songchen 松岑. "Lun xie qing xiao shuo yu xin she hui zhi guan xi 论写情小说与新社会之关系 [On the Relationship between Love Stories and New Society]." Eds. Chen, Pingyuan 陈平原 and Xia, Xiaohong 夏晓红. *Er shi shi ji Zhongguo xiao shuo li lun zi liao* 二十世纪中国小说理论资料 *[Theoretical Materials on Chinese Novel in the Twentieth Century]*. Beijing: Beijing da xue chu ban she, 1989.

Spivak, Gayatri Chakravorty. *Outside in the Teaching Machine*. New York: Routledge, 1993.

Stowe, Harriet Beecher. *Uncle Tom's Cabin*. New York: Random House, 1985.

Sun, Ge 孫歌. "Xu yan 序言 (Preface)." *Yu yan yu fan yi de zheng zhi* 語言與翻譯的政治 *[Language and the Politics of Translation]*. Ed. Xu Baoqiang 許寶強 and Yuan Wei 袁偉. Hong Kong: the Oxford University Press, 2000, vii-xxxii.

Taisho shinshu Daizokyo 大正新修大藏經. Vol. 55. Tokyo: Taisho shinshu Daizokyo Kankokai, 1960-1978.

Tang, Xiaobing. *Global Space and the Nationalist Discourse of Modernity : The Historical Thinking of Liang Qichao*. Stanford, Calif.: Stanford University Press, 1996.

Tarumoto, Teruo. "A Statistical Survey of Translated Fiction 1840-1920." In *Translation and Creation: Readings of Western Literature in Early China, 1840-1918*. Ed. David Pollard. Amsterdam and Philadelphia: John Benjamins Publishing Company, 1998.

Toury, Gideon. "Translated Literature: System, Norm, Performance: Toward a TT-Oriented Approach to Literary Translation." *Poetics Today* 2.4 (1981): 9-27.

Tsai, Benjamin. *Enemies of the Revolution: Ideology and Practice in Making of Chinese Liberalism 1890-1927*. Diss. University of Chicago, 2000.

Tytler, Alexander Fraser. *Essay on the Principles of Translation*. Amsterdam Studies in the Theory and History of Linguistic Science: Series I, Amsterdam Classics in Linguistics; V. 13. Amsterdam: J. Benjamins, 1978.

Venuti, Lawrence. *The Scandals of Translation: Towards an Ethics of Difference*. London and New York: Routledge, 1998.

Waley, Arthur. "Notes on Translation." *The Atlantic Monthly* 100 (1958): 69.

Wang, Der-wei David. *Fin-De-Siecle Splendor : Repressed Modernities of Late Qing Fiction, 1849-1911*. Stanford: Stanford University Press, 1997.

Wang, Guoliang 王國良. *Wei Jin Nanbei chao zhi guai xiao shuo yan jiu* 魏晉南北朝志怪小說研究 [A Study of Zhi guai fiction of Wei, Jin, and Southern and Northern Dynasties]. Taibei: Wen shi zhe chu ban she, 1984.

Wei, C. X. George and Yang, Xiaoyuan, ed. *Chinese Nationalism in Perspective: Historical and Recent Cases*. Westport: Greenwood Press, 2001.

Wei, Weiyi. "Wo de fu qin --- Wei Yi 我的父亲——魏易 (My Father --- Wei Yi)." In *Lin Shu Wei Yi he yi xiao shuo quan ji chong kan hou ji* 林纾魏易合译小说全集重刊后记 (*Postscript of the New Edition of the Complete Translations by Lin Shu and Wei Yi*. Taibei: Wei Weiyi, 1990: 96-111.

Willcock, Hiroko. "Meiji Japan and the Late Qing Political Novel." *Journal of Oriental Studies* 33.1 (1997): 1-28.

Wu, Rulun 吴汝纶. *Wu Rulun quan ji* 吴汝纶全集 [*Completed Works of Wu Rulun*]. Hefen: Huangshan chu ban she, 2002.

Wu, Zhuoliu 吴浊流. *Yaxiya de gu er* 亚细亚的孤儿 [*The Orphan of Asia*]. Beijing: Ren min wen xue chu ban she, 1986.

Xia, Xiaohong 夏晓红. *Wan Qing nü xing yu jin dai Zhongguo* 晚清女性与近代中国 [*Late Qing Females and Modern China*]. Beijing: Beijing da xue chu ban she, 2004.

Xiong, Yuezhi 熊月之. *Xi xue dong jian yu wan Qing she hui* 西学东渐与晚清社会 [*The introduction of Western Learning and Late Qing Society*]. Shanghai: Shanghai ren min chu ban she, 1994.

Xue, Shuizhi 薛绥之 & Zhang Junchai 张俊才, ed. *Lin Shu yan jiu zi liao* 林纾研究资料 [*The Study Materials About Lin Shu*]. Fuzhou: Fujian ren min chu ban she, 1982.

Yamada, Keizo. "Han yi 'Jia ren qi yu' zong heng tan 汉译佳人奇遇纵横谈 (On Chinese Translation of Kajin No Kigu)." *Zhongguo gu dian xiao shuo xi qu lun ji* 中国古典小说戏曲论集 (*Selected Papers on Traditional Chinese Fiction and Drama*). Ed. Zhao Jingshen. Shanghai: Shanghai gu ji chu ban she, 1985. 384-403.

Yan, Fu 严复. *Yan Fu ji* 严复集 [*Works of Yan Fu*]. 5 vols. Ed. Wang Shi 王栻. Beijing: Zhonghua shu ju, 1986.

Zhang, Guoqin 張國慶. "Zhui xun Taiwan yi shi de ding wei 追尋台灣意識的定位 In search of Taiwanese Identity." *Zhong wai wen xue* 中外文學 (*Chinese and Foreign literatures*) 23.10 (1995): 102-26.

Zhang, Taiyan 章太炎. *Zhang Taiyan xuan ji* 章太炎选集 *[Selected works of Zhang Taiyan]*. Shanghai: Shanghai ren min chu ban she, 1981.

Zheng, Hailing 郑海陵. *Wen xue fan yi xue* 文学翻译学 *[Literary Translatology]*. Zhengzhou: Wen xin chu ban she, 2000.

Zheng, Zhenduo 郑振铎. *Zhongguo wen xue yan jiu* 中国文学研究 *[Studies on Chinese Literature]*. 3 vols. Beijing: Zuo jia chu ban she, 1957.

Zhou, Zuoren 周作人. *Zhongguo xin wen xue de yuan liu* 中国新文学的源流 *[The Origins of New Chinese Literature]*. Shanghai: Huadong Normal University Press, 1995.

Zhu, Xizhou 朱羲冑. *Chunjue zhai zhu shu ji* 春覺齋著述記 *[Accounts of Works in the Studio of Awakening Spring]*. Shanghai: Shi jie shu ju, 1949.

Zhu, Zhiqing 朱自清. *Shi yan zhi bian* 诗言志辩 *[Anaylysis of "Poetry Speaks of the Intentions"]*. Beijing: Gu ji chu ban she, 1956.

Zou, Zhenhuan 邹振环. "Zhongguo jin dai fan yi shi shang de Yan Fu yu Wu Guangjian 中国近代翻译史上的严复与伍光健 [Yan Fu and Wu Guangjian in the Translation History of Modern China]." *1993 nian Yan Fu guo ji xue shu yan tao hui lun wen ji 1993* 年严复国际学术研讨会论文集 *[1993 Yan Fu International Conference Proceedings]*. Fuzhou: Hai xia wen yi chu ban she, 1993. 527.